ARMY OF NONE

Strategies to Counter Military Recruitment, End War, and Build a Better World

Aimee Allison and David Solnit

Seven Stories Press
New York | Toronto | London | Melbourne

A Seven Stories Press First Edition

Seven Stories Press
140 Watts Street
New York, NY 10013
www.sevenstories.com

In Canada: Publishers Group Canada, 559 College Street, Suite 402, Toronto, ON M6G 1A9

In the UK: Turnaround Publisher Services Ltd., Unit 3, Olympia Trading Estate, Coburg Road, Wood Green, London N22 6TZ

In Australia: Palgrave Macmillan, 627 Chapel Street, South Yarra, VIC 3141

Library of Congress Cataloging-in-Publication Data

Allison, Aimee.
Army of none : strategies to counter military recruitment, end war, and build a better world / Aimee Allison and David Solnit. — 1st ed.
p. cm.
ISBN-13: 978-1-58322-755-8 (pbk. : alk. paper)
ISBN-10: 1-58322-755-5 (pbk. : alk. paper)
1. United States—Armed Forces—Recruiting, enlistment, etc. 2. United States—Armed Forces—Recruiting, enlistment, etc.—Iraq War, 2003- 3. War resistance movements—United States. 4. Iraq War, 2003—Protest movements—United States. 5. Afghan War, 2001—Protest movements—United States. I. Solnit, David. II. Title.

UB323.A648 2007
355.2'23620973—dc22 2006037812

College professors may order examination copies of Seven Stories Press titles for a free six-month trial period. To order, visit: www.sevenstories.com/textbook or send a fax on school letterhead to (212) 226-1411.

Printed in Canada

9 8 7 6 5 4 3 2 1

Back cover photo: US Marine Corps Drill Instructor and his platoon of "Young Marines" at Marine Corps Air Station Cherry Point, North Carolina. Camera Operator: LCPL Andrew Pendracki, USMC, 2003.

BOOK DESIGN BY JASON JUSTICE ★ WWW.JUSTICEDESIGN.COM

To those seeking peace and justice—

a better world begins at home.

ARMY OF NONE

TABLE OF CONTENTS

Introduction

SECTION ONE

SECTION TWO

COUNTERRECRUITMENT 67

TABLE OF CONTENTS

Photo: Camera Operator: LCPL NICHOLAS J. GALVIN, USMC, 2004

Acknowledgments

Aimee Allison

Love and gratitude to my husband Aaron and son Isaiah for supporting me during many struggles for a more peaceful world. Heartfelt thanks to my friend and mentor Elmaz Abinader, who nurtured my written voice and showed me the way. And appreciation to the remarkable people who have dedicated their lives to countering recruitment and militarism including Susan Quinlan, Arlene Inouye, Rick Jahnkow and countless parents, teachers and youth.

David Solnit

Much appreciation to Jen Angel and my sister Rebecca Solnit for assistance and support. Thanks to Crystal Yakacki of Seven Stories for her efforts. Gratitude to friends from the People Powered Strategy Network for work co-developing and popularizing people power antiwar strategy: Doyle Canning, Jet Heiko, Orin Langelle, Anne Petermann, Sue Hilderbrand, Antonia Juhasz, Charles, Meddle Bolger, Patrick Reinsborough, and David Meieran.

ABOUT THIS BOOK

So, you and some friends have decided to get military recruiters out of your local school or community. You should know that you join a powerful and growing movement that is directly challenging the recruitment and militarization of youth. Counterrecruitment organizing is the most practical way to tangibly resist United States policy that, while cutting funding for education, employment, and social programs, promotes war and empire. It exposes the relationship between, and acts to correct, both local and global injustices. As counter-recruiter Rick Jankow of Youth And Non-Military Opportunities (YANO) in San Diego puts it, "The argument is based on simple but compelling logic: The Bush administration and conservative-dominated Congress can continue to ignore antiwar demonstrations and other symbolic forms of protest, but they cannot ignore the fact that without enough soldiers, it is impossible to sustain a large, long-term occupation in a country like Iraq."[1]

Since the advent of the current wars in Iraq and Afghanistan, counterrecruitment work has run the gamut from one-on-one counseling sessions to street-side poetry slams to citywide lobbying efforts. We wrote this book in order to help you build a successful counterrecruitment movement in your community. *Army of None* begins by arming you with information about the aggressive military recruitment happening in public schools, on college campuses, and throughout communities. It then offers the strategies, tools, and resources you need to creatively and effectively act against military recruitment and reclaim your school, community, and future.

WHY WE WROTE THIS BOOK

Aimee Allison

Once, during one of my regular visits to a small public high school near my house, I met Marissa,[2] a young woman who was excited and fearful about life after graduation. Like many of the other students at her school, she was the daughter of a poor immigrant family and had come up through difficult circumstances.

But she was articulate, composed, bright, and ambitious. She wanted a better life and was willing to work for it. She'd taken the initiative as a middle-school student to find an alternative to the large, impersonal, and oftentimes violent high school in her district. She'd embraced a self-directed internship program in psychology and had taken courses at the local community college. She'd been accepted into university.

In a better world this young person would be rewarded for pulling herself up by her bootstraps and overcoming incredible odds to make a better future for herself and her community. She would have a full scholarship to pursue her dreams. Instead she was planning to join the military—they promised her $40K for college. She dreamed of becoming a psychiatrist and was promised a similar position in the Army. Marissa's decision to join was not based on politics or morality. It was a simple matter of economics.

Marissa takes me back nineteen years to when I was a young bootstrapper myself who believed that I could accomplish anything if I worked hard enough. When the recruiter sized me up, as they are trained to do, he saw a woman just dying to break out of her shell, to succeed.

I joined the Army the spring of my senior year, when the ink on my acceptance letter to Stanford was still fresh. My parents couldn't help me pay for school, but the recruiter, who had a desk in the career center and had been my mentor, promised that the military would make my dreams come true.

When I looked into Marissa's eyes I saw myself, and I knew that the best way to discuss joining the military was to tell the story of my experience as a soldier. As we sat together that afternoon, I told her about how I never received the $20K in loan repayments that they'd promised me. I told her about how I didn't make the money I thought I would—that if I'd worked at McDonalds, I could have made more and at least been able to quit when something better came along. I told her about how they made me cut my hair short, remove my braces, cover my tattoo, and take off all of my rings.

I told her about chanting "Kill the people, burn the village" while marching over five miles with hundreds of other women and about how that chant still runs through my veins to this day, even though I was raised by my family and church to believe that killing is wrong. I told her about how my hospital unit went to the Persian Gulf to deal with the over one hundred suicides by American soldiers that occurred in less than four weeks. And how poorly the government treats veterans, as I witnessed in the cramped hospital rooms in the Palo Alto Veterans Affairs medical facilities.

I told her how "Stop Loss" keeps soldiers in the service even after they have honorably served their time. How being deployed will interrupt her studies and how there are many soldiers headed to Iraq for the third time in four years—imagine being a college freshman at twenty-two. About how I met a young woman paralyzed at the age of twenty-three from a roadside bomb in Iraq and how she now has to sleep in the living room of her mom's house because her wheelchair doesn't fit through any other door.

I told her about how one in three young women in the military endures harassment, sexual abuse, and/or rape—and that I was one of them. About how my drill sergeant tried to take advantage of me. About what it's like to be a woman in a male world, where rank is everything and you can't have it. About what it's like to be a person of color (and half of the enlisted women in the military are African American) in an oppressive system that feels the closest to slavery of all I that have experienced.

After all that, shared not in a preachy way but in a respectful "did you know?" kind of way, she had questions. Like, how could what you are telling me be so different from what I see in the ads—and from my talks with the recruiter? I explained that recruiters only give one side of the story because their goal is to get you to sign up. But, I continued, you need much more information to make the right decision for yourself. I told her that since I was in the military and am a veteran, I could help her to make an informed decision. Perhaps you should wait and do a bit more research before signing the bottom line? Perhaps we could go to the Foundation Center in San Francisco to look for more scholarships—I'll take you. Perhaps we can review the financial aid package again and see if you can pick up work study, or more loans. I told her, don't be afraid of loans—it's the best investment that you can make for yourself. I told her that despite joining the Army, I ended up paying for my Stanford education on my own. Just sent in my last payment in November of 2004, and I jumped up and down and screamed, "I did it!" to my dog.

This is what counterrecruitment looks like. A conversation. Some information. My arm around a young, confused person trying to do right. Some stories to balance out the $4 billion in slick ads that suggest to this young lady that the military can offer her freedom and a future. Our conversation ended the way they all do—Marissa is going back to the drawing board (with my help) to find other ways to pay for school and to live her best life.

David Solnit

In high school I thought that my friends and I were going to be drafted into the United States military and sent to fight a war for oil in the Middle East. It was 1979. The Vietnam War and the military draft had ended just a few years before. Americans waited in long gas lines and United States military intervention in the Middle East was openly discussed, as oil producing countries banded together in OPEC, setting off an "oil crisis." The Carter administration had drawn the Soviet Union into invading Afghanistan and was recruiting, arming, and training the anti-Soviet guerrilla army, led by Osama bin Laden, that would later become the Taliban.

Meanwhile the all-volunteer army was in crisis. It could not meet recruiting goals. President Jimmy Carter announced that he would bring back registration for a military draft, which had been canceled at the end of the Vietnam War.

It was at about this time that Michael Stoops, a community organizer, came to my high school and participated in a debate with a military recruiter. He told us about a citywide group of high school students from all over Portland that was forming to oppose draft registration and a draft. I went to a meeting and joined. We organized against President Carter's draft registration. We planned pickets and concerts with antiwar speakers, and chanted, "Hell No, We Won't go, We Won't Die for Texaco!" We talked to other high-school kids. We got the Portland school board to pass a resolution against the draft.

Initially motivated to resist being forced into the United States military to fight for oil and empire with others of my generation, I was ultimately motivated by the idea that regular people could make change to improve our lives, our communities, and the world. I had been successfully recruited into the movement for justice and fundamental change.

A few years later my slightly younger cousin, restless, and done with high school, planned to join the military—he wanted to be a Navy Seal. I wrote him (old school: pen on paper in an envelope with a stamp in the mailbox) a long letter warning him of all the reasons I had learned of why it might be a mistake to join. When I saw him last year—twenty-five years later—he told me that my letter persuaded him not to join. Instead he became one of the youngest smokejumpers in the country, parachuting out of helicopters to fight wildfires. Now much older, he is just about to get his nursing degree.

Sending that letter to my cousin was my first counterrecruiting experience. Talking with youths, families, and communities about the realities and implications of joining the military can also be a positive act of inviting people to join the movements for justice and a better world. It's become absolutely clear to me that our counterrecruitment and antiwar efforts are absolutely essential steps away from war, empire, and injustice and toward that better world.

TEN REASONS FOR COUNTERRECRUITMENT

As a part of the counterrecruitment movement you can:

1. Support student and youth leadership.
2. Bring veterans to the forefront.
3. Meet the needs of poor and working-class youth.
4. Effectively challenge the teaching of military values.
5. Help build long-term relationships between teachers, parents, community groups, veterans and students.
6. Effectively challenge war and empire.
7. Discover and create alternatives to military values, war, and empire.
8. Affect citywide, nationwide, and international efforts for peace and justice.
9. Build communities committed to social, economic, and political justice.
10. Take concrete action that feels good.

COUNTERRECRUITMENT FOR A BETTER WORLD

If you are a big tree, we are a small axe.
—Jamaican proverb

Ready to create a truly grassroots, people powered movement? Antiwar activism is changing. The familiar sights and sounds of large protests are giving way to quieter, but far more resonating, one-on-one work in classrooms, career centers, and communities. Whenever you hear people decry the lack of large-scale protest in the United States, even as the latest polls show more than 60 percent of people are opposed to the current war in Iraq, remember that the model for effectively challenging war is taking a different shape.

People from all walks of life are finding inspiration and success in working locally to educate students and mobilize against military recruitment where it happens. We can see counterrecruitment asserting itself as a viable movement as independently organized actions in Seattle, Austin, and Los Angeles contribute to a national context in which public schools around the country limit military recruiter access, a huge success by any measure. Schools and communities are now considering deeper questions about the increasing militarization of our culture and recognizing the need for schools to teach and weave peace into the minds and aspirations of our children.

We believe that a hundred thousand marching one day every six months is not as effective as one thousand people talking to students every day.

In January 2006 The National Security Advisory Group, which includes former Secretary of Defense William Perry and former Secretary of State Madeleine Albright, issued a report entitled *The U.S. Military: Under Strain and at Risk*. The report predicted a major recruiting crisis, pointing out that fewer than needed recruits, as well as first time enlistees, could result in a "hollowing" and imbalance in the Army. The fact is, at the end of 2005, the active Army fell 6,627 recruits short of its annual goal of 80,000. In addition, the Army Reserve fell 16 percent behind its recruiting target for the year, and the National Guard 20 percent short of its annual goal.[3]

Today approximately 9,000 soldiers are not permitted to leave the service because of "stop-loss" orders, which retain soldiers on active duty involuntarily after their period of enlistment is complete. Another 2,000 soldiers have been involuntarily recalled after leaving active Army service. Despite this compulsory service, the Army Reserve has trouble achieving its target numbers.

After the 2005 recruiting disaster, the military pulled out all stops in an effort to "make quota" in 2006. Army brass replaced Army Recruiting Command's top officer in October 2005 with Stanford-educated Major General Thomas Bostick. "A lot of concerns, I think, that the parents and applicants have are about Iraq and Afghanistan," Bostick told the *Tampa Tribune* in October 2006.[4] They also replaced Leo Burnett, their lead public relations agency who created the "Army of One" campaign, with Mcain Erickson who after a 200 million dollar contract and year of research came up with "Army Strong" as the new recruiting slogan.

In their comprehensive new strategy, the military added 1,200 new recruiters and spent millions on a public relations blitz that included TV ads, video games, Web sites, cell phone text messages, helicopter simulators in the back of 18-wheelers, internet chat rooms, sports and public event sponsorships, and even ads on the ticket envelopes for Greyhound Bus lines ("This ticket will take you to where you are going, but the National Guard will take you to where you want to be"). The Army also increased its relationship with NASCAR, the National Hot Rod Association, and the Professional Bull Riders Association. The plan calls for recruiters to visit schools and malls a few days before an event, offering free tickets and the chance to meet famous drivers or bull riders.[5]

In addition, the military dramatically lowered their educational and test standards and other qualifications. The U.S. Army recruited more than 2,600 soldiers under new lower aptitude test standards in 2006. They allowed neck and hand tattoos, increased the allowable age to 42, increased the enlistment bonus up to $40,000 and offered $1,000 to soldiers who persuaded friends to sign up. They have granted an unprecedented number of "moral character" waivers; around 17 percent of the first-time recruits, or about 13,600, were accepted under waivers for various medical, moral or criminal problems, including misdemeanor arrests and drunk driving. But even that was not enough to "meet quota."[6]

So, they also lied. From 2004 to 2005 the Government Accounting Office found 6,600 allegations of recruiter crimes.[7] Incidents included concealing medical information that would disqualify a recruit; making false promises and helping recruits get around test requirements. In 2006 the pressure was even greater, and seen in an ABC television investigation from November 2, 2006, that sent undercover students into ten recruiters' offices in New York and New Jersey. The program reported that more than half of the recruiters were "stretching the truth or even worse, lying." They found, "nearly half of the recruiters who talked to our undercover students compared everyday risks here at home to being in Iraq." A Patchogue recruiter was caught saying. "You have a 10-times greater chance of dying out here on the roads than you do dying in Iraq."

It also reported that, "some recruiters told our students if they enlisted there was little chance they'd go to war. One recruiter told a student his chances of going to war were "slim to none."[8]

After all this, the military claims to have met it's 2005-2006 goals of recruiting 80,000 people to fill it's ranks. They have provided no independent verification of their alleged statistics, but they have launched major public relation effort to counter the bleak news from the year before.

The *Armed Forces Journal* reported in March, 2006, that recruiters "face an increasingly reluctant pool of potential recruits, opposition from antiwar protesters and perennial bureaucratic inefficiency in the recruitment system."[9] Scrambling in all of these ways to meet their numbers, the Army, more than ever before, needs fresh blood—recruits straight out of high school.

Is Counterrecruitment Just a Way to End the War in Iraq and Afghanistan?

Counterrecruitment is not simply a tactic to end the wars in Iraq and Afghanistan. It is a broad-based, strategic approach to challenging the roots of unending war and militarization. The full potential of a progressive peace and justice movement will only be realized when there is an observable link between efforts to stop war and efforts to address inequality in class, race, ethnicity, immigration status, and other socioeconomic factors that determine who ends up being sacrificed in our government's wars. As recent statistics demonstrate, there are limits to how far Bush and the neocons can go with their plan for global hegemony when the resources for it are running dangerously low. Fortunately, the peace movement is in a position to further diminish those resources.

If we apply ourselves to countering military recruitment, it is in our power to both limit the government's capacity to wage new wars and build a stronger base to challenge the nation's spending priorities. Simply put, counterrecruitment is a strategic and effective way to challenge the prowar, antieducation priorities of our government.

Wouldn't a Draft Create the Movement We Need?

Practicing effective self-government and democracy requires that we instil in individuals a propensity for critical, creative thinking and a willingness to challenge the "chain of command" when institutions are not serving their needs. Bringing back the draft is the opposite of what we should do to achieve those goals.

—Rick Jahnkow, counterrecruitment leader.[10]

Some people concerned about military recruitment and the war think only a draft will get average Americans involved in stopping the wars in the Middle East.[11]

Contrary to common belief, there are three types of military drafts in the United States. The first type includes "stop loss" measures, often referred to as a backdoor draft, that keep military members in the service involuntary after their contract is up. Then there is the poverty draft, whereby the poorest in the country are drafted into war via aggressive and underhanded recruitment and a lack of alternatives.

While the standard draft of the Vietnam War does not exist at this moment, eighteen-year old young men have been required to register for selective service since the 1980s. The standard draft can be implemented in seventy-five days.

It was certainly true during the Vietnam War that this kind of draft mobilized the resistance. "In many ways," says Vietnam-era student activist Dan Siegel, "the antidraft movement overcame the anti-Vietnam War movement. People were concerned about their own skins but didn't work to stop the U.S. war machine longer term."[12] Vietnam-era activists often decry the fact that forty years after their work, the United States is in the same violent cycle as before. The anti-draft movement didn't result in the sustained change necessary.

To achieve this kind of sustained change, we must do more than say no to the draft, regardless of its form. We must say no to all the adverse effects war has on our communities. We must make connections between injustice abroad and at home, and tie in local struggles with global ones. The counterrecruitment movement is convincing more and more Americans that the war in Iraq is not supportable and certainly not the answer for young people looking for educations and jobs. The movement is convincing more and more Americans that young people looking for educations and jobs are better beneficiaries of our tax dollars than those who profit from unjust war. To the extent that counterrecruitment can enhance and expand the types of alternatives available to young people, the downward trend for military recruiters will continue. It is only in creating something new than we may dismantle the old.

Reaping Seeds Sown During Vietnam Era

Of course there were more sustainable antiwar strategies developed during the Vietnam era that inspired modern counterrecruitment. Their strength lies in making connections between the social struggles for equality at home and the war. Dr. Martin Luther King, Jr., eloquently spoke to the relationship between peace and civil rights:

> Then came the buildup in Vietnam, and I watched [the poverty] program broken and eviscerated, as if it were some idle political plaything of a society gone mad on war, and I knew that America would never invest the necessary funds or energies in rehabilitation of its poor so long as adventures like Vietnam continued to draw men and skills and money like some demonic destructive suction tube. So, I was increasingly compelled to see the war as an enemy of the poor and to attack it as such.[13]

The same year of Dr. King's speech, student and community activists organized the country's first counterrecruitment actions, called Stop the Draft Week. According to organizer Dan Siegel, its purpose was, "To cut off the supply of recruits to the military in Vietnam . . . to raise awareness of the draft and its impact on working class communities and particularly working class communities of color." They adopted the theme, "From Protest to Resistance." If being in the streets couldn't stop the war, staying out of uniform certainly could.

A convergence of antiwar and social-justice organizations challenged the system that used people of color and the poor as cannon fodder. It created a coalition of directly impacted ethnic minority groups. In fact, the Black Panthers had a large membership of returning

Vietnam Vets who were angry at having supposedly fought for Vietnamese civil rights while being denied their own back home. Likewise, the Chicano Moratorium was the largest antiwar group in Southern California and consisted largely of veterans and civil rights workers. At its heart the roots of the counterrecruitment movement are ethnically diverse, focused on the poor and disenfranchised, driven by veterans and military families, and organized to affect systemic change both locally and globally.

The government responded with stepped-up police repression, violence, and surveillance. In California, Stop the Draft Week organizers led three thousand marchers to the Oakland induction center on October 16, 1967. When demonstrators refused orders to leave, police attacked them with nightsticks, injuring twenty. On the second day demonstrators returned, and ninety-seven were arrested. On the third, ten thousand arrived, this time retreating from the police, successfully blocking streets as they departed. Then, as now, dismantling the mechanisms that turn people into soldiers was deeply threatening to the system.

War and Empire

As U.S. Marine Corps Major General Smedley Butler put it in 1933, "There are only two things we should fight for. One is the defense of our homes and the other is the Bill of Rights. War for any other reason is simply a racket."[14] Racket is one term, empire is another to describe why the U.S. government spends $441 billion a year[15] on a military of over two and a half million soldiers[16] (2,685,713 with reserves)[17] and why it has more than 700 military bases spread across 130 countries with another 6000 bases in the United States and its 'territories.'[18] Understanding what military recruits are used for in the world, understanding war, and creating viable alternatives to both are essential if we want to break out of the deadlock of militarism.

Since the collapse of the "other superpower," the Soviet Union, "empire" has become a common term among both critics and advocates referring to the unparalleled U.S. system of economic, political, cultural, and military domination of the world. The *New York Times Magazine* ran a 2003 cover story titled "The American Empire (Get Used to It.)" describing the U.S. as a reluctant, but benevolent global empire. While Bush claimed in his 2004 State of the Union speech, "We have no ambitions of empire," months later Karl Rove snapped at a *New York Times* reporter: "'We're an empire now, and when we act, we create our own reality."[19]

Some see the start of American empire in the wake of Second World War or after the collapse of the Soviet Union in 1989. Others trace it back to the invasion and conquest of numerous indigenous nations in North America from the seventeenth century onward, the development of a slave economy with tentacles reaching into Africa, and the 1848 seizure of Mexico's northern half that is now the Southwest. Another wave of aggression abroad began in the twentieth century. Smedley Butler describes the U.S. military's role in this emerging empire, "I served in all commissioned ranks from Second Lieutenant to Major-General. And during that period, I spent most of my time being a high-class muscleman for Big Business, for Wall Street, and for the Bankers. In short, I was a racketeer, a gangster for capitalism."

The modern-day version of "war as a racket" and gangsterism for capitalism can be seen in the occupation of Iraq. Critics call the United States war in Iraq a failure, but behind the scenes it has established several permanent U.S. military bases, allowed corporations like Halliburton to make billions from unfulfilled contracts to reconstruct war-destroyed schools, hospitals, power systems, and infrastructure, and is in the final process of turning control of Iraq's vast oil resources over to war profiteers such as Chevron. The U.S. occupation's "Provisional Authority" under Paul Bremer also laid the legal groundwork for much of the Iraqi economy to be privatized and then taken over by U.S.-based corporations. Thus Butler's racket and its toll abroad. What does it cost us at home?

The price of two and a half million soldiers, aircraft carriers and military bases across the planet, and a massive array of weapons of mass destruction is high. It saps resources for healthcare, education, and housing. It also requires keeping the domestic population in check through propaganda and the corrosion of civil liberties and human rights. Stifling domestic dissent, criminalizing immigrants, and torturing and illegally imprisoning citizens of other nations have all been stepped up under the guise of the so-called War on Terror. In his book, *The Empire Has No Clothes: U.S. Foreign Policy Exposed*, Ivan Eland writes, "intervention overseas is not needed for security against other nation-states and only leads to blowback from the one threat that is difficult to deter—terrorism. In short, the U.S. Empire lessens American prosperity, power, security and moral standing. It also erodes the founding principles of the American Constitution." As we write this book (late 2006) nearly 3,000 US soldiers and over 200 soldiers from other occupying countries have been killed in Iraq, at least 20,895 U.S. troops have been wounded, and a new Johns Hopkins report puts the number of violent Iraqi civilian deaths since the 2003 invasion at more than 600,000. War's side effects are bleak for the environment and human society; its direct and intended effect is mass death. Down the current road of imperial dominance and warfare at will, the use of weapons of mass destruction is nearly inevitable, with apocalyptic consequences.

But there are alternatives to the expense of maintaining a military and the atrocity that is war. One that has been developed over the last fifty years is called social defense. Brian Martin, Australian scholar and author of *Social Defense: Social Change,* describes social defense as unarmed "community resistance to aggression as an alternative to military defense. It is based on widespread protest, persuasion, non-cooperation and intervention in order to oppose military aggression or political repression. There have been numerous nonviolent actions, to be sure, some of them quite spectacular, such as the Czechoslovak resistance to the 1968 Soviet invasion, the toppling of the Marcos dictatorship in the Philippines in 1986, the Palestinian intifada from 1987–1993 and the collapse of communist regimes in Eastern Europe in 1989."[20] Imagine if even a fraction of the resources put into military defense were available for the general population to organize social defense.

Replacing global empire with domestic democracy and well-being requires re-defining democracy—pursuing ways to shift decision-making and power from corporations and government to "we the people." It's not enough just to oppose something. We need to envision, educate about, and then actually organize alternatives to the system of empire and war, to corporations, and to the lack of democratic participation in decisions that shape our lives and communities. What begin as pragmatic actions, like keeping youth from joining the military, are most effective when they have as their end the transformation of the root causes of war, undemocratic governance, and injustice. Every immediate action, when understood and explained as part of a bigger picture, can be another step toward this longer-term goal of getting to the roots of our problems and building a better world.

Today's Movement

Counterrecruitment is not just "saying no" to the military. Students need support, affirmation, guidance, job skills, hope, and confidence that they can do it.
—Arlene Inouye, Founder, Coalition Against Militarism in our Schools[21]

Arlene Inouye, who began her activism during Vietnam, continues her work today in the Los Angeles Unified School District, where she founded the Coalition Against Militarism in our Schools (CAMS). Her support of a bright young student named Sal illustrates how counterrecruitment works simultaneously to resist war and to build alternatives. Arlene says, "Sal is a bright JROTC student who lacked support for success in school and beyond. His father was deported to Mexico about two years ago, and he was told by the military-recruiter that if Sal enlisted, his father could come back to the U.S. His father begged him to enlist after high school. Sal later learned that the military was lying and that he couldn't help his father come home."

During the spring of 2006 there were student walkouts and marches supporting immigrant rights throughout Los Angeles. Arlene explains, "The activism around immigrant rights helped Sal to see the hypocrisy of fighting in a military that is being sent to the border and has been reported to shoot down undocumented people who try to cross.

"During a rally, Sal took off his JROTC uniform in front of the press, encouraging other students to resist war and drop out of JROTC. Unfortunately, most won't because of concerns about their grades. This student who is articulate and smart is failing school, and lacks the support he needs. I have mobilized help for him at the school and call him regularly. He just got back from a peace camp given by our partner organization, and that was a powerful experience for him." Creating a supportive community to enable Sal's dissent, and help him forge an alternative path, is at the heart of counterrecruitment. As demonstrated by Sal's example, the best movement is as much about envisioning and building a new world as it is about resisting the injustices of this one.[22]

SECTION ONE

MILITARY RECRUITMENT

US Marine Corps Sergeant verbally "fixes" a Marine Recruit, while conducting an inspection drill at Marine Corps Recruit Depot, Parris Island, South Carolina.
Photo by: LCPL BRYSON K. JONES, USMC, 2004

THE MILITARY MESSAGE AND THE FACTS

"Your son mentions enlistment and a million things rush through your head. We're hoping one or two of these things are facts."

"Talking with your daughter about the military has you anxious and emotional. It's times like this, facts are reassuring."

"Your son is looking for guidance on one of the biggest decisions he will ever make. This is no time to find yourself at a loss for words."
—Department of Defense recruitment web site[23]

Top Military Recruitment Facts:

1. Recruiters lie. According the *New York Times*, nearly one of five United States Army recruiters was under investigation in 2004 for offenses varying from "threats and coercion to false promises that applicants would not be sent to Iraq." One veteran recruiter told a reporter for the *Albany Times Union*, "I've been recruiting for years and I don't know one recruiter who wasn't dishonest about it. I did it myself."[24]

2. The military contract guarantees nothing. The Department of Defense's own Enlistment/Re-enlistment Document states, "Laws and regulations that govern

military personnel may change without notice to me. Such changes may affect my status, pay allowances, benefits, and responsibilities as a member of the Armed Forces REGARDLESS of the provisions of this enlistment/re-enlistment document" (DD Form4/1, 1998, Sec.9.5b).

3. Advertised signing bonuses are bogus. Bonuses are often thought of as gifts, but they're not. They're like loans: If an enlistee leaves the military before his or her agreed term of service, he or she will be forced to repay the bonus. Besides, Army data shows that the top bonus of $20,000 was given to only 6 percent of the 47,7272 enlistees who signed up for active duty.[25]

4. The Military won't make you financially secure. Military members are no strangers to financial strain: 48 percent report having financial difficulty,[26] approximately 33 percent of homeless men in the United States are veterans, and nearly 200,000 veterans are homeless on any given night.[27]

5. Money for college ($71,424 in the bank?). If you expect the military to pay for college, better read the fine print. Among recruits who sign up for the Montgomery GI Bill, 65 percent receive no money for college, and only 15 percent ever receive a college degree.[28] The maximum Montgomery GI Bill benefit is $37,224, and even this 37k is hard to get: To join, you must first put in a nonrefundable $1,200 deposit that has to be paid to the military during the first year of service. To receive the $37k, you must also be an active-duty member who has completed at least a three-year service agreement and is attending a four-year college full time. Benefits are significantly lower if you are going to school part-time

From "Mixed Signals," a counter-recruitment tool in comic book form. Available to activists, teachers and others, from peacecomic@yahoo.com

or attending a two-year college.[29] If you receive a less than honorable discharge (as one in four do), leave the military early (as one in three do), or later decide not to go to college, the military will keep your deposit and give you nothing. Note: The $71,424 advertised by the Army and $86,000 by the Navy includes benefits from the

Army or Navy College Fund, respectively. Fewer than 10 percent of all recruits earn money from the Army College Fund, which is specifically designed to lure recruits into hard-to-fill positions.[30]

6. Job training. Vice President Dick Cheney once said, "The military is not a social welfare agency; it's not a jobs program." If you enlist, the military does not have to place you in your chosen career field or give you the specific training requested. Even if enlistees do receive training, it is often to develop skills that will not transfer to the civilian job market. (There aren't many jobs for M240 machine-gunners stateside.)

7. War, combat, and your contract. First off, if it's your first time enlisting, you're signing up for eight years. On top of that, the military can, without your consent, extend active-duty obligations during times of conflict, "national emergency," or when directed by the President.[31] This means that even if an enlistee has two weeks left on his/her contract (yes, even Guard/Reserve) or has already served in combat s/he can still be sent to war.[32] More than a dozen U.S. soldiers have challenged "stop-loss" measures like these in court so far, but people continue to be shipped off involuntarily.[33] The military has called thousands up from Inactive Ready Reserve—soldiers who have served, some for as long as a decade, and been discharged. The numbers: twice as many troops are fighting in Iraq and Afghanistan per year as during the Vietnam War. One-third of the troops who have gone to Iraq have gone more than once. The highest rate of first-time deployments belongs to the Marine Corps Reserve: almost 90 percent have fought.[34]

The above was excerpted and adapted from *The New Yorkers' Guide to Military Recruitment in the 5 Boroughs*.[35]

- "The objective of the School Recruiting Program Handbook is to assist recruiters with programs and services so they can effectively penetrate the school market. The goal is school ownership that can only lead to a greater number of Army enlistments."[36]

- "The Armed Services Vocational Aptitude Battery Test (ASVAB) is designed to provide the field recruiters with a source of prequalified leads . . . The ASVAB recruiter printout provides information you can't get from any other list. It . . . provides the recruiter with concrete and personal information about the student.

- The first purpose of financial education incentives is "to encourage college-capable individuals to defer their college until after they have served in the military."[37]

—From the military's recruiter training manual, "The School Recruiting Program Handbook" (United States Army Recruiting Command (USAREC) Pamphlet 350-13).

US Air Force (USAF) personnel assigned to the 317th Recruiting Squadron let children play with "Ricky the Recruiter" Mascot.
Camera Operator: TSGT JIM VARHEGYI, USAF, 2001

THE MILITARY'S GOAL: Own the School

STUDENTS:

Just knowing that Uncle Sam is trying to trick you into joining the military will help you resist the heavy pressure.

Only 10 percent of recruits initiate the recruitment process. Family and friends (known to the military as "influencers") are increasingly discouraging enlistment.[38] In response, the military employs systematic, inventive methods to pull students in—methods that parents may not be aware of. The military spent $3.9 billion on a wide variety of recruitment activities in 2006. Effective counterrecruitment activities must address their type, timing, and location.

Privileged Campus Access for Military Recruiters

The most blatant indication of military recruiting on campus is the regular presence of uniformed recruiters. In many schools recruiters have unchecked access—unlike most adults and organizations, which must schedule appearances in campus cafeterias and classrooms. Recruiters pull students from class and take them out to lunch, or to other off-campus activities, without their parents' permission. The school bureaucracy can either help or hinder these efforts. Many counterrecruitment campaigns are aimed at changing the way that rules are observed. This can make a big difference.

School Counselors and Recruitment

School counselors are the first line from the military to the student. They have the power to allow recruiters a space in the career center, to arrange special military career days, and to point them toward particular students. They can require students to take the Armed Services Vocational Aptitude Battery test (ASVAB), assign Junior Reserve Officer Training Corps (JROTC) classes, or guide students into military clubs like the Young Marines. Likewise, they have the power to offer space for nonmilitary options in the career center, tell students about the risks and myths of joining the military, require students to sign up before meeting with a recruiter, and welcome counterrecruitment tabling on career night.

The story of Brian Moss,[39] a career-center liaison at a large Midwestern high school, sheds light on school counselors' crucial role in the recruitment process. He'd built strong relationships with the recruiters. "They're the nicest people I've met," he boasted. For many years he'd welcomed all services—fourteen recruiters in all—to the school as often as they'd like. He especially talked up the Coast Guard to the kids he counseled—he felt it was a terrific opportunity.

One day a local community person who'd made some counterrecruitment presentations in classes gave the counselor a packet of information that included a copy of the actual enlistment contract, the film *Arlington West*, and some counterrecruitment pamphlets for students considering enlistment. Reading the language of the military enlistment contract changed Brian's mind about promoting the military option to his students. Section 9b reads, "Laws and regulations that govern military personnel may change without notice to me. Such changes may change

Air Force Master Sergeant training supervisor, 3506th US Air Force Recruiting Group, updates the recruiting production board. Camera Operator: MSGT MIKE DIAL, 1985

my status, pay, allowances, benefits, and responsibilities as a member of the Armed Forces REGARDLESS of the provisions of this enlistment/reenlistment document." Section 10d2 reads, "I may be ordered to active duty for 24 months, and my enlistment may be extended." In other words, the military enlistment contract isn't a real contract.

PARENTS/COMMUNITY MEMBERS:

Counselors can wrongly assume that military style coercion and a culture of domination is the solution for "at-risk" youth, particularly poor or minority youth. Don't accept it. There are many ways for young people to learn respect, self-discipline, and scholarship. Find alternative programs in the area and educate counselors about their options.

The military does not legally have to honor its promises to the enlistee. That was enough to change this counselor's opinion of the service. By the following year he had become an ally to counterrecruiters working on campus. He started passing out counterrecruitment literature to students and changed career-center rules so that recruiters were required to make appointments with students in order to meet with them on campus.

Militarizing Youth

Story: Sal Garcia

Sal Garcia began his military career in the seventh grade when his East Los Angeles middle-school counselor recommended that he attend Angel Gate Academy boot camp to deal with his disciplinary and academic problems. The camp is described on its web site as a "Short-term residential and educational program for at-risk youth from the Los Angeles Unified School District aged 11–14."

Sal Garcia (pictured on left) with teacher and fellow high school activists at a counterrecruitment event. Photo: Arlene Inouye, Coalition Against Militarism in our Schools.

"My father wasn't the best father in the world. He gave me a lot of problems," Sal explains, "I was picked on a lot in school. I wasn't the most popular kid at school and then I had to go home to deal with my family."

Cpl. Korey Smith, 15, (right) of Easterns Junior ROTC program, awaits orders from the team commander during drill practice. Louisville, Kentucky. Photo: Geoff Oliver Bugbee

He describes his experience as a twelve-year-old in boot camp:

> The second we got off the bus after an eight-hour ride, the Army personnel was in our faces screaming. Kids were crying. They taught us how to march 100 percent like the Army. We did chants just like the Army. We slept just like the Army. We had to learn the Army rank structure. We learned to do the salute. All we did was physical, there wasn't any education. We always had to drink a glass of water and if we didn't, they would throw it over our heads. Every kid felt they had been recruited into the Army—we really got into the military mindset.
>
> Even though my grades were still bad, the first thing I told my counselor when I got back was 'Put me in Cadet Corps,' which is the middle-school version of ROTC. They took the group of eighth-grade Cadet Corps members to Arena Elementary to try to get the fifth-graders to sign up for Cadet Corps. They were like, 'Wow, you guys are cool!' We would get medals for recruiting them into Cadet Corps. I ended up enrolling in ROTC for high school, too.[40]

Amber Crawford, 16, ranking major in Eastern High School's ROTC program leads fellow cadets (left to right) Jessica Roberts, 15, Michelle Jarboe, 15, and Casey Story, 17, through drill proctice in the gymnasium hallway during sixth period. Louisville, Kentucky.
Photo: Geoff Oliver Bugbee

The JROTC program

JROTC is one of the best recruiting devices that we could have.
—then Secretary of Defense William Cohen, February 2000

Over half a million students are sitting in JROTC classes in any given day learning about civics and values from military perspective. Responsibility and self-discipline can be taught in many ways. This one has dangerous implications.
—Rick Janhkow, Committee Opposed to Militarism and the Draft

- Number of students currently enrolled in JROTC programs: 500,000
- Percentage of JROTC cadets who are recruited into the lowest enlisted military ranks: 50 percent
- Percentage of JROTC cadets who are youth of color: 54 percent
- Average JROTC annual operating cost paid for by local school districts: $76,000[41]
- Average cost to school district for an after-school tutoring program: $40,000
- Average length of time military pays for costs of JROTC programs: 1–3 years[42]
- Subjects required to be taught in JROTC program: None[43]

The Junior Reserve Officer Training Corps (JROTC) is promoted to school districts as an educational and leadership-training program. It claims to keep "at-risk" students from dropping out, though there is no proof that it does.

The "leadership" training is actually intensive recruitment of low-income youth enticed by excellence, comradeship, and patriotic zeal. School districts offer physical-education credits for JROTC courses. If other gym classes become full, counselors have been known to enroll students into such classes without their parents' permission.

MILITARY RECRUITMENT

As we write this, our fourteen-year old friend Theo, an incoming ninth-grader at a high school in Oakland, California, just discovered that he was assigned to a JROTC class despite his and his mother's objections. An immigrant family from Tonga, Theo's family will need strong assistance from those familiar with the school system to force the school to change his schedule.

A recruitment program based on early contact, JROTC is embedded in high schools across the country. Instead of preparing young officers, JROTC helps recruit the lowest-level military ranks. The curriculum of JROTC brings a discriminatory policy toward LGBTQ (Lesbian, Gay, Bisexual, Transgender and Queer) people, violence as conflict resolution, and weapons training into schools. The curriculum is designed by the Pentagon and regulated by national JROTC Cadet Command—never by local school boards, principals, or teachers. Military instructors are not required to have college degrees or credentials for the subjects that they teach.

JROTC students at San Diego area high schools perform drills with wooden rifles. Photo: Rick Jahnkow, Project on Youth and Non-Military Options.

Story: Dayana Cardoso

Dayana Cardoso was immediately attracted to JROTC during class registration day her freshman year at her San Pedro, California, high school. "The students were at the booth and were wearing the uniforms. They talked about working out together and learning good skills. I just really wanted to be part of something. I signed up for it that day." It turned out the structure, physical demands, and ability to advance fit in with Dayana's personality and drive. "I made first lieutenant my first year, which is a really high honor," she explained.

Throughout her years, she did more than just attend JROTC class. She was junior varsity captain of the drill team, proudly led her unit in parades and events, and even traveled on a field trip to Edwards Air Force Base to help Military Police-training practice riot control techniques. She wanted everyone to love JROTC as much as she did. "I didn't like the fact that some kids were forced into JROTC because they ran out of PE classes. They wouldn't participate in the pushups, running, or drilling which messed it up for the rest of us."

But Dayana's life changed when she heard that a peace club formed on campus. "I went to a meeting my sophomore year, just to argue with the people. They were saying, 'We should help out people in those countries,' and I said, 'They are terrorists.' We all learned about the terrorists in JROTC." The next year Dayana went back to the peace club, but this time she sat in the back of the room and just listened. She learned that the military contract is actually eight years, not the four years she'd been told by her JROTC instructors. "I asked myself, how come they didn't tell us that? If they are giving me all this, what is the catch?" So she started going to meetings and educating herself about the Iraq War. By the end of her junior year she was peace club president.

"I really like the way that ROTC functions—the way they show you discipline, and you are able to be an authority in an organization. I liked doing community involvement like car washes to raise money to help veterans." But the new information she learned led her to begin asking questions during JROTC class. "I guess I got on their nerves, especially since I'd been put in a leadership position. But I didn't support what recruiters were doing, and I knew that JROTC isn't like real military life."[44]

Dayana thinks that if the peace club weren't at the school, she would have tried to get into one of the military academies. Her JROTC instructor encouraged her to join the National Guard. As it turned out, Dayana stopped JROTC the first semester of her junior year and now is headed for college in Hawaii.

Seneca JROTC Battalion Commander Lt. Col. Joe Sabel, 18, left, and Major Dana Chesser, 17, right, inspect cadet Matt Ernst, 17, on the shooting range during a sixth-period JROTC class. Louisville, Kentucky. Photo: Geoff Oliver Bugbee

The Price of JROTC

According to a publication by the Central Committee for Conscientious Objectors, "The military offers schools a package deal that sounds too good to be true—at first. But as soon as people take a good hard look at the program, they find themselves asking more and more questions. Do they want a military recruitment program inside the school district? Do they want to violate their own anti-discrimination policies to get it? And do they want to pay for it when so many other programs are being cut?"[45]

A recent online article reported the findings of the Michigan-based Military Service Dialogue Committee, a project for the Institute of Global Education (IGE). In 2004 the group embarked on a study of the military presence of JROTC in public schools and investigated Grand Rapids Public Schools:

> We decided to focus on GRPS because it houses the only JROTC program in Kent County and because we assumed the JROTC affected the numbers recruited in the city high schools. Our information was received in writing after several meetings and questions to the previous Superintendent of Grand Rapids Public Schools, Bert Bleke. We were interested to learn about JROTC curriculum qualifications and pay of JROTC instructors, total cost to the district, numbers of enrollees and were somewhat startled by the information we gleaned.
>
> The federal government determines salaries of the retired Army instructors, so the JROTC instructors are plugged into the school district's eighteen-step pay scale based on the federal predetermined pay rate. The step they have achieved, therefore, does not necessarily have any relationship to their educational achievement or years of teaching experience. In 2004–5 the four JROTC teachers' salaries totaled

> $488,160! Their supervisor who works on a fifty-two week contract was paid $76,000. The entire budget for JROTC-GRPS for that year totaled over $500,000. Certain estimated benefit costs and revenue from the government had reduced the total budget from $698,000. Our committee was amazed at the cost of this program.[46]

Arlene Inuoye, founder of the Coalition Against Militarism in our Schools (CAMS), describes the JROTC in the Los Angeles Unified School District, and what her local counterrecruitment coalition is doing about it:

> In LAUSD, there are thirty high schools that offer JROTC as a physical education elective at a cost of over $3 million. The 6,000 students enrolled in the JROTC classes come from predominately poor and working-class communities of Latinos and African Americans. At Roosevelt and across the city, students are often involuntarily placed into JROTC because of a lack of physical education electives. Even when students ask to be changed, they remain in JROTC for months. Why? Is it because there are not enough physical education classes to which to transfer them in these overcrowded schools? Why is JROTC expanding nationally, across the district, and at Roosevelt, while other classes have been slashed or received reduced funding?
>
> We have signed petitions to ax JROTC programs, presented concerns to the Board of Education, and documented cases on students involuntarily placed into the class and cases in which students have been misinformed about the program. We have distributed literature and facts about the program.[47]

JROTC is sold to school districts as a "free" program. Too often, school boards and school administrations sign on the dotted line before the truth sinks in: that JROTC comes with big costs. The Department of Defense contributes a relatively small portion of the overall financial burden—it's school districts underwriting the cost of teaching young people to march, drill, and learn military history and behavior. And the military's initial offer is a one- to three-year special, after which the costs go up significantly. Under the standard JROTC contract, the Department of Defense provides students with books, uniforms, and "special equipment," such as rifles. Insurance, building facilities, and maintenance, half the salaries, and all benefits; all of these are costs to the district. Again, when the Pentagon approaches a school board, it often presents quite different figures and may lower the costs for the first few years.

Even with "sweetener deals" and special extra subsidies offered to new units, schools cannot avoid the basic arithmetic: the contract requires them to hire two military retirees for up to 150 students. In the course of a normal school day most high school teachers teach between 150 and 200 students by themselves. Thus schools are, from day one, paying more for JROTC than for science, math, reading, history, and other academic subjects and far more than for physical education (for which JROTC is often substituted).[48]

In DeKalb County, Georgia, school officials estimated $6,500 per school in nonpersonnel expenses, ranging from phone calls and transportation to special field trips to local military bases. They also estimated $56,000 in start-up costs for the district's fifteen units, including classroom renovation and secure storage facilities for weapons and uniforms.[49] Some branches of the military require the districts to pay for uniform cleaning and equipment maintenance.

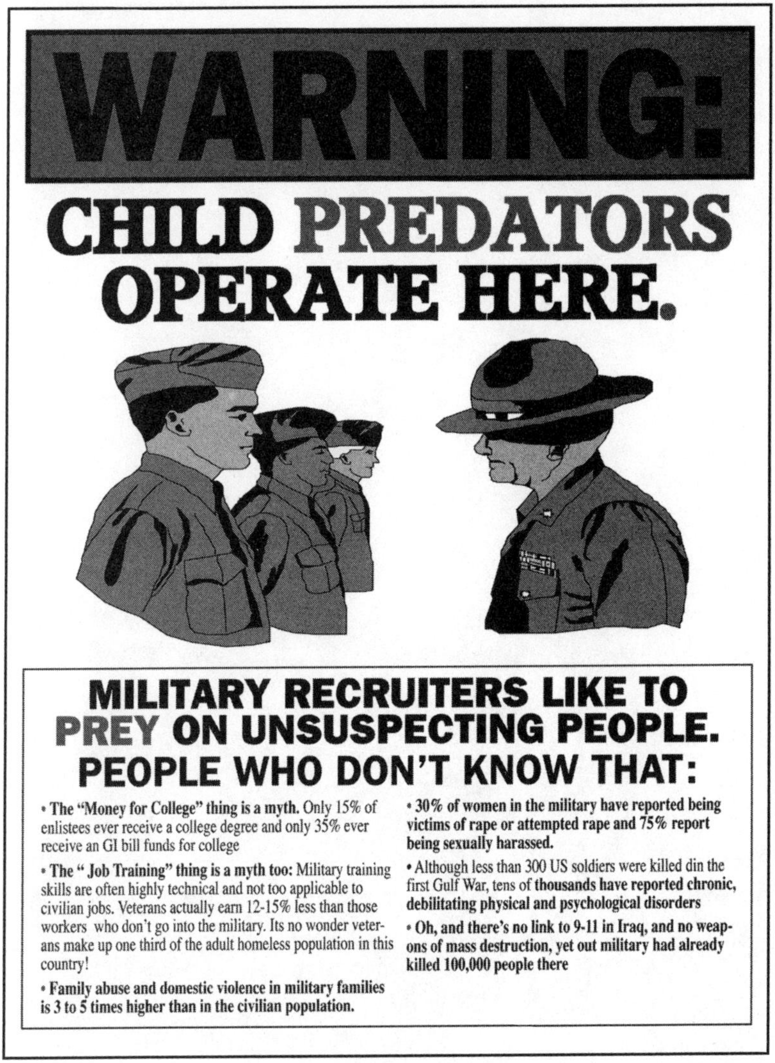

In Washington, DC, school officials have chosen to wipe out conflict resolution and cut deeply into dropout prevention programs while expanding JROTC. In other districts, foreign languages, arts departments, and other programs essential to young people's education and self-esteem are being slashed in the face of tightening budgets. School-to-work, mentorship, urban gardening, job training,

oldamericancentury.org

multicultural understanding, conflict resolution—these programs build leadership and career skills for all students, not just for those who choose the military option. Most of all, these civilian-run programs *belong* in our schools, and are true part of what it means to educate our young people.[50]

A sample of JROTC's net cost to some school districts across the nation:

City	Net Annual Cost	Annual Cost Per Unit
Atlanta, GA	$1.5 million	$136,000
Prince George's County, MD	$1.1 million	$55,000
District of Columbia	$799,910	$61,531
San Francisco, CA	$570,000	$71,250
New York, NY	$368,000	$36,000
Cottage Grove, MN	$82,021	$82,021[51]

Partnerships/Adopt A School

PARENTS:

The military is not relying solely on JROTC or military recruiters to have access to your child. Pleasant-sounding "Adopt A School" programs actually bring children in direct contact with more military life, and at a younger age, than you might imagine possible.

Many elementary and middle-school districts have official partnerships with military units—a link that gives the military easier access to students through school-sponsored events. As many as 350 Army units have adopted local schools all over the country as part of the Partners in Education initiative. The Markham Elementary School in Fort Belvoir, Virginia, for example, welcomes soldiers from the local United States Army Intelligence Security Command into their cafeterias as buddies for lunching students. They also run a pen-pal program.[52]

Military partners routinely take young children on field trips to military bases or appear in the classroom or on campus in uniform. In effect, young students are being taught military values and groomed for recruitment long before high school.

Horton Elementary School in San Diego County had a partnership with the Navy Sea Control Squadron VS33. During Christmas time a National Guard recruiter came to the school dressed as Santa Claus and handed out bags full of military recruitment swag—including military-embossed pens and book covers. Later that year the unit arranged for a tank to be driven on to the school campus for a "career fair" that included only military options. Parents voiced their opposition and the school relented and promised it would not happen again.[53]

PARENTS/COMMUNITY MEMBERS:

Do you know if your neighborhood schools have partnerships with the military? Search your school district's web site for partnerships or Adopt A School for a list, or simply call the school principal.

Young Marines

Nothing like watching an army of eight-year-olds goosestepping to the tune of a sadistic DI to make you feel all warm and fuzzy about being an American . . .

—Henry Chinaski, responding online to a blog about Young Marines[54]

- Number of youths 8–18 in Young Marines units: 10,000
- Number of Young Marines after-school programs: 240[55]
- Number of on-campus arrests of children for violations of "zero tolerance" policies that include bringing toy guns to school: 3.1 million[56]

Young Marine units are popping up all over element-ary and junior high school campuses. Often the after-school program directly asks school personnel for help in advertising and promoting the club. The Young Marines are an officially sponsored program of the Marine Corps, self-described as "a youth education and service program for boys and girls aged eight through completion of high school" that serves to "promote the mental, moral, and physical development of children." To join a Young Marines unit, children must complete a thirteen-week boot camp.[57] Many parents are resisting the Young Marines units settling in their child's school site because of the highly militarized rituals of the program. The children wear camouflage uniforms and march with realistic-looking toy rifles. The adult leaders expect complete obedience and command the club members as soldiers. One blogger, Henry Chinasky, commented that "I actually watched these 'young marines' being marched in formation with a drill instructor scream-ing in their faces during a parade outside Twenty-Nine Palms . . . Actually, I was instantly reminded of the Hitler Youth (another military organization devoted to the teaching of responsibility and 'moral character')."[58]

Data Mining: Recruiting Databases

- Number of student records in files mandated by No Child Left Behind: 4 million youths per class year: 90 percent of high school age population
- Number of records in Pentagon's database of 16 to 25 year-olds: 30 million

- Number of School Districts in U.S.: 16,540[59]
- Total numbers of high school students at Los Angeles Unified School District: 63,000
- Number of Los Angeles Unified School District students that opted out in 2004: 8,000
- Number of Los Angeles Unified School District students that opted out in 2006: 18,000[60]

Beware—military recruiters can, without your knowledge, obtain your private information gathered from many sources, including the ASVAB test, the No Child Left Behind Act, and data collected by the Pentagon database from My Space profiles, teen magazines, class ring companies, raffles, your classmates, and many other unexpected sources.

If you're a student in a high school or college, the military is tracking your moves. Contact data is regularly released to military recruiters. Once they have the data, you will routinely get phone calls, texts, mailings, or surprise visits. They will bombard and try to sell the military to you, based on your favorite hobby or brand of jeans. Like football? Well, you could play football in the Army. Oh, you're a musician? Play in the Navy band. Like cute boys? Well, the military is just full of 'em.

Pentagon Database

Since 2002 the United States Department of Defense has spent $500 million as part of the Joint Advertising, Marketing Research & Studies (JAMRS) project creating an illegal data base of thirty million 16 to 25 year-olds that includes over 700 pieces of information including students' contact information, ethnicity, email address, family information, school information, grades, activities, work and college information, and much more. The Pent-

The No Child Left Behind Act:

SEC. 9528. ARMED FORCES RECRUITER ACCESS TO STUDENTS AND STUDENT RECRUITING INFORMATION.

(a) POLICY

(1) ACCESS TO STUDENT RECRUITING INFORMATION

Notwithstanding section 444(a)(5)(B) of the General Education Provisions Act and except as provided in paragraph (2), each local educational agency receiving assistance under this Act shall provide, on a request made by military recruiters or an institution of higher education, access to secondary school students names, addresses, and telephone listings.

(2) CONSENT

A secondary school student or the parent of the student may request that the student's name, address, and telephone listing described in paragraph (1) not be released without prior written parental consent, and the local educational agency or private school shall notify parents of the option to make a request and shall comply with any request.

agon claims that it is "arguably the largest repository of 16 to 25 year-old youth data in the country." The goal of the database is to help give the Pentagon's $3.8 billion recruiting budget maximum impact.[61]

Operation Opt Out: A Counterrecruitment Tactic to Protect Student Privacy

Operation Opt Out is a strategy to inform high school students of their legal right to keep their private information from being released to military recruiters. There are two separate databases that students should opt out of if they don't want the military to use the information to target them for recruitment: the high school recruitment list that districts are required by the No Child Left Behind Act to deliver, and the Pentagon's huge database on youth.

Students may legally opt out of the both databases by handing in forms to the school district that move the student's information to a "suppression file." The Pentagon retains the information in both databases but does not release it. Many groups were successful in 2005–2006 in pushing up the rates of opt outs in schools across the country.

Recruiters begin requesting the student lists in early October. You have a short window in the late summer and fall to encourage students and their families to submit their opt out forms to the district. Although opt out campaigns are not a cure-all for military recruitment, they can be an important part of an overall strategy because they make students and parents aware that military recruiters are obtaining and releasing their information. They also support and encourage students to take action and assert their legal rights. A tool to automatically generate opt out letters for both NCLB and the pentagon database can be found at www.leavemychildalone.org.

TIPS:

- Hand out opt out forms and information in English and Spanish (if applicable) before school and during class.
- Go beyond the regular school day; pass opt out forms during class registration, back-to-school nights, and school orientations and parent meetings.
- Post information about opt out rights where students and parents frequent. Think about grocery stores, laundromats, cafés.
- Measure results: compare the number of students who opt out year after year.

School- or district-level changes are also possible. Opt out campaigns have been very successful in school districts across the country, and have resulted in best-practice policies that range from putting the opt out checkbox on the required emergency contact form to only requiring only one form for the entire high school career instead of one each year.

To protect privacy at the city level, the Leave My Child Alone Adopt A School Board Kit offers guidance in getting your local school board to adjust its policies to support student privacy as it relates to releasing info to recruiters. The kit can be downloaded from www.themmob.org/lmca/lmca_forms/schoolboard_kit.pdf.

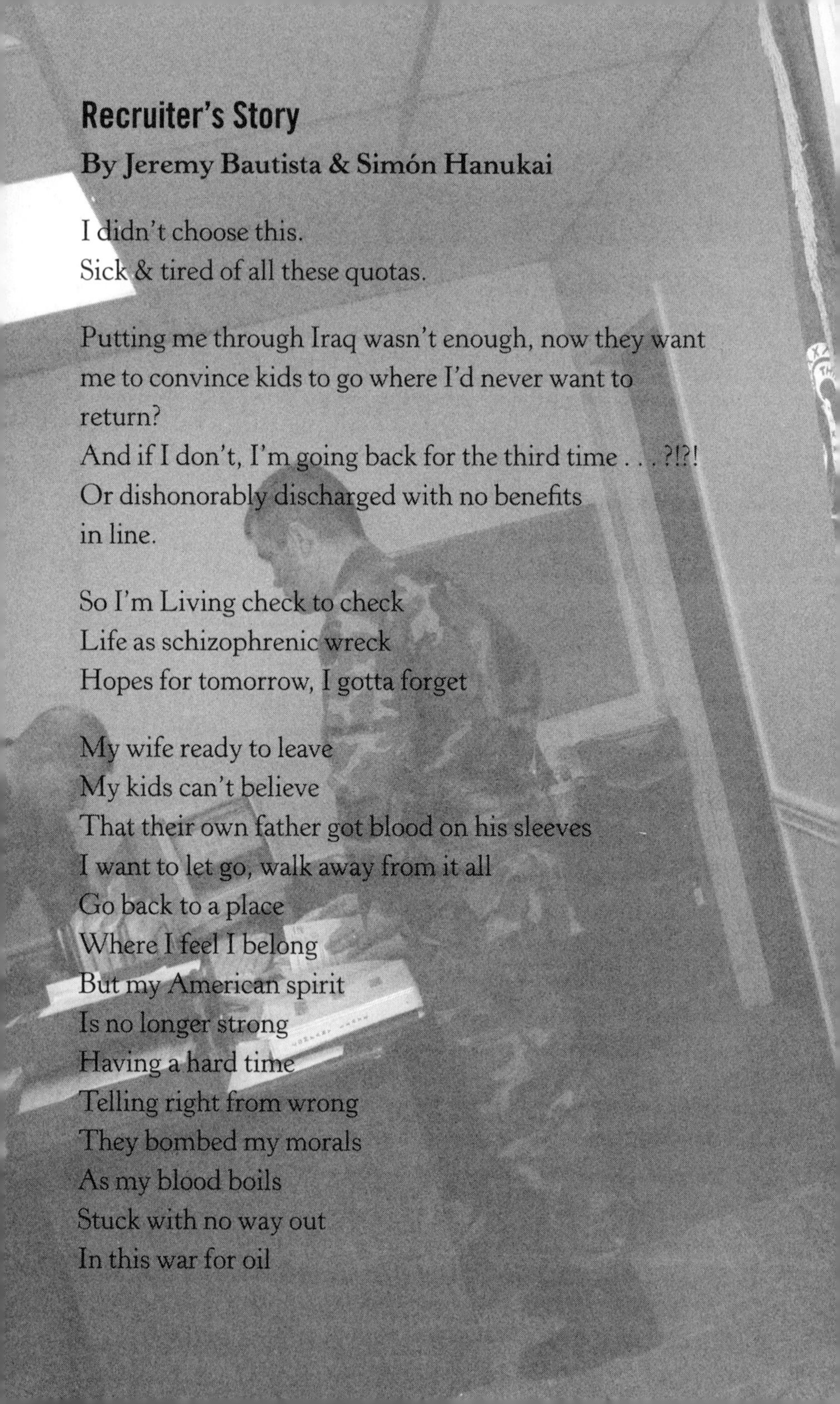

Recruiter's Story

By Jeremy Bautista & Simón Hanukai

I didn't choose this.
Sick & tired of all these quotas.

Putting me through Iraq wasn't enough, now they want
me to convince kids to go where I'd never want to
return?
And if I don't, I'm going back for the third time . . . ?!?!
Or dishonorably discharged with no benefits
in line.

So I'm Living check to check
Life as schizophrenic wreck
Hopes for tomorrow, I gotta forget

My wife ready to leave
My kids can't believe
That their own father got blood on his sleeves
I want to let go, walk away from it all
Go back to a place
Where I feel I belong
But my American spirit
Is no longer strong
Having a hard time
Telling right from wrong
They bombed my morals
As my blood boils
Stuck with no way out
In this war for oil

I'm not a bad guy.
Yet I must go on telling these lies

Instead of sending kids beyond borders
I'd rather be saving lives in Mississippi corridors

A casualty of choice, that's all I am and
ever will be, a pawn of the US military . . .

A large-as-life cardboard cutout soldier adorns the interior of this Army Recruiting office. Photo: Geoff Oliver Bugbee

Story:
No Child Left Standing in Marin County, California

In 2005, responding to their sophomore history class assignment to "change the world," David Crawford and fellow Tamalpais student Paul Coach researched the little-known provision of the federal No Child Left Behind Act and how it impacted their middle-class high school community. What they found out shocked them enough to inspire a "No Child Left Standing" campaign that had a tangible and important impact on their North Bay town. David Crawford explains:

> We found out that Tam High gets $245K a year in Title One federal funding which equals one twenty of our budget. If we said no to the military's request for information we would have to cut a librarian and all after-school tutoring. In nearby Richmond and Oakland districts, title one funds make up to eight tens of their budget. Imagine what would happen in those schools.
>
> I'm a student trustee, and in one meeting the principal told me that the military had come by asking for student data. He had only one month to comply. My friend and I were scared—why is the military coming here? Only half of the school had opted out at that point. We put together a campaign to inform kids about their rights. We didn't talk about our campaign as promilitary or antimilitary, it's about informing students about their rights. We got the opt out forms, put together a web site, held up posters, and distributed information with Redwoods Seniors for Peace at 7am in front of the school for two weeks. We talked to kids we never met before.

Over 450 students returned the opt out forms in two weeks. That year 950 of 1150 students opted out. We can show the military that even the school couldn't say no, we can opt out, which is the same as saying no.

We didn't stop there. We looked at the Tamalpais District registration packet and found out that the opt out was this tiny box on one of thirty pages. We went to the school board, and after some debate got them to mail a letter home along with the opt out form. On top of this, in December 2005 we also got them to approve a resolution that says, "We, the members of the Tamalpais School Board, do not believe that section 9528 of the No Child Left Behind Act, requiring schools to turn over student contact information to the military recruiters, should be included in the NCLB. The board supports the troops in the United States Armed Forces, but does not believe that the threat of withholding federal funding unless student information is given to recruiters is appropriate for a Federal law that is specifically focused on education.

It just shows that a couple of teens from Tam High can make a difference.

Armed Services Vocational Aptitude Battery (ASVAB) Test

. . . From the recruiter's perspective, the ASVAB is not only a valuable tool used to maintain and improve school relations but it is also specifically designed to provide recruiters with a source of prequalified leads. The ASVAB recruiter printout provides information you can't get from any other list. It

gives the recruiter the students' Armed Forces Qualification Test scores, military aptitude composites, and career goals. It identifies the best potential prospects for recruitment that allows recruiters to work smarter.
—Army publication, USAREC Pamplet 350–13[62]

- U.S. schools that offer ASVAB: ⅔
- Number of schools per year that allow the military to get around opt out by giving the ASVAB: 14,000[63]
- Number out of 39 Los Angeles Unified Schools that didn't release ASVAB data to recruiters: 2
- Students who take the ASVAB test are asked to sign a privacy waiver granting the military recruiter access to contact information, social security number, gender, and race. (See www.afsc.org/youthmil/militarism-in-schools/ASVAB.htm)

The Armed Services Vocational Aptitude Battery (ASVAB) is marketed to schools as a career aptitude test for high school students. The aptitudes it measures are specifically aligned with military jobs. I was excused from two class periods in high school to take the ASVAB test. The test measured manual dexterity and ability to follow direction. The on-campus recruiter looked at the results and listed the five jobs I was eligible for.

Most often, school administration allows students to leave normally scheduled classes to take the test during school hours. Students, most of them under age, must sign a release to get the results. The release form requires contact information that is used by recruiters to follow up with the test takers.

Even if a school offers the ASVAB, the recruiters don't have to get any juicy contact information from it. The principal or school counselor can choose Option 8 when arranging to have the test given at the school. Option 8

An unidentified U.S. Marine Corps (USMC) Recruit armed with a M16 rifle, equipped with a combat bayonet, executes a straight thrust on the practice dummy during his bayonet assault course. Marine Corps Recruit Depot, Parris Island, South Carolina.
Camera Operator: SSGT JOHN A. LEE II, USMC, 2004

Marine recruits sit during processing at Marine Corps Recruiting Depot, Parris Island, South Carolina.
Camera Operator: LCPL CHAD H. LEDDY, USMC, 2003

protects students' privacy and parental rights by allowing for the test, but not permitting information to be used for recruitment purposes. Some counterrecruiters have convinced principals to offer the test only on a Saturday as another tactic to limit the test to those who really want to take it. Another approach is to have students fill in the school's address and phone number, so that information received by recruiters doesn't violate the students' privacy.

STUDENTS:

Most people do need help in thinking through the careers and life we would like. Many career-counseling tests are available. The ASVAB measures a person's ability to do military jobs and is not designed to give a full range of career options to students. The best bet is not to take the ASVAB and to find another tool; just Google "career assessments" for links to a number of free career tests.

The Military in the Classroom: Channel One

- Number of middle schools and high schools showing Channel One every school day: 11,000
- Number of students who watch the twelve-minute program: 7 million
- Average number of advertisements per broadcast: 4
- Average number of military ads per broadcast: 2[64]

Channel One is required viewing in over ten thousand classrooms every school day. In the middle of domestic and international news programs, there are ads—half of them from the military. For years, the military has purchased time on the Channel One program in order to directly reach twelve- to-eighteen-year-olds. Parents are often shocked to learn that their children see military commercials every day. One such parent, Dr. Teresa Whitehurst, writes, "Nobody asked for my consent before exposing my daughter to military recruiting ads at her public school, where I *thought* she was getting an education, not getting into the hands of military recruiters. But times have changed, and so have our schools."

Dr. Whitehurst recommends calling the school to ask if Channel One is being shown with military-recruiting commercials and arranging a personal visit to see the programming. She continues, "It's your right to watch this 'news' program to see what your children are being exposed to at school, where violent ways of handling conflicts (whether interpersonal or international) should not be taught, and where safety from seduction and harassment ought to come first."[65]

Magazines

Many districts carry the preteen magazine *Cobblestone,* aimed at children ages nine to fourteen. The May 2006 issue, featuring a cover photo of a soldier in Iraq clutching a machine gun, included articles on what it's like to go through boot camp, a rundown of the Army's "awesome arsenal," and detailed descriptions of Army career opportunities. A set of classroom guides that accompany the magazine suggest that teachers invite a soldier, Army recruiter, or veteran to speak in their classes, and asks students whether they might want to join the Army someday. One sixth-grade teacher told the *Boston Globe* that the guides look exactly like the official recruiting material distributed at high schools.[66]

Recruiting Outside of the School Day

In those Army ads, when they go home with their uniforms on, it's really cool. He's going home. He's not going in jail, or dead. That's really cool.
—Alfredo Alatorre, high school senior[67]

Nobody has mentioned killing, or being killed. Iraq remains a far-off land. Another perfect recruitment day.
—LA Weekly[68]

Actual Greyhound Bus ticket holder envelope.

America's Army Videogame

In its quest to find recruits, the military has literally turned war into entertainment.
—Sheldon Rampton, "War is Fun as Hell"[69]

You have this gigantic Hummer in a tent loaded with guns, a rotatable turret, and a huge screen in front of it. Jinx took

the wheel and drove us around this virtual war zone while shooting people with a pistol, and I switched off from the SAW turret on the top of the vehicle to riding passenger with an M4.

—"Eekers" describing her turn at "Combat Convoy Experience" on the *America's Army* web site blog[70]

- Number of registered users of the United States Military's video game *America's Army*: 6,000,000
- Cost to develop: $12 million
- Chance that a four-to-six-year-old U.S. boy plays video games every day: 1 in 4

America's Army offers a range of games that kids can download or play online. They provide a fantasy version of military culture, training, and weaponry. According to the September 2006 *Businesswire*, "While *America's Army* is probably best known as the creator of one of the five most popular PC action games played online, with almost seven million registered users and over 2,000 game servers, it was initially built as a recruiting tool and originated in the U.S. Army's Office of Economic Manpower & Analysis."[71] In the latest version, "Special Forces (Overmatch)" offers realistic simulations that are played alone or with other registered users.

The games are presented as simulations, such as Javelin training, where players "learn how to employ the Army's first true 'Fire and Forget' Anti-Armor weapon" and the "Virtual Recuiting Station," where players can meet veterans from the War on Terror. The *America's Army* web site features a "U.S. Army" link that leads to the recruitment text, "There over 200 different jobs in the U.S. Army; each called a

Military Occupational Speciality (MOS). More than ever before, the knowledge and experience an MOS offers will help you build the confidence, skills, and character to last a lifetime. To learn more about the many different opportunities available: visit goarmy.com."[72]

In "War is Fun as Hell," author Sheldon Rampton writes about how *America's Army* is more than just another violent video game, it is the basis for a culture of militarism and glorifying violence in youth. "Ubisoft, the company contracted to develop the DoD's games, also sponsors the 'Frag Dolls,' a real-world group of attractive, young women gamers who go by names such as 'Eekers,' 'Valkyrie,' and 'Jinx' and are paid to promote Ubisoft products. At a computer gaming conference earlier this year, the Frag Dolls were deployed as booth babes at the *America's Army* demo, where they played the game and posed for photos and video (now available on the *America's Army* web site)."[73]

Adventure Vans

Military "Adventure Vans" and other specially outfitted vehicles tour the country with weapons simulators, high-tech video presentations, and cadres of highly trained recruiters who present themselves as educators.

Events Marketing

The United States military is now using events to create its image or "brand" and to reach potential recruits. A cover story in *Event Marketer* magazine recently noted, "The world's most powerful army is also one of the leanest, meanest event marketing machines around. Live marketing campaigns are infiltrating events across the nation to connect with prospects and rebrand the Army as cool, high-

Recruiter from Atlanta West Recruiting Station.
Camera Operator: SUSAN NORVICK, CIV, 2001

Students protesting an Army Cinema Van visiting their high school campus. Photo: Arlene Inouye, Coalition Against Militarism in our Schools.

tech, smart, and happenin'." The article continues, "The Army has created no less than ten major event programs: sponsorships of the National Hot Road Association, the Arena Football League, and NASCAR; the proprietary All-American Bowl; mobile college and football tours, a two-market Spring Break program; participation in third-party events; a fleet of H2 Hummers competing in custom car shows; and an effort touring the fair and festival circuit. All Army events feature brand messaging, supporting visuals, and on-the-ground interactives that facilitate leads."[74]

US Air Force Major General Stephen G. Wood swears in new recruits, who are on the delayed enlistment program, during the opening ceremonies of the 2004 NASCAR race at the Las Vegas, NV, Motor Speedway. Camera Operator: SRA BRIAN FERGUSON, USAF

BRAND ARMY: Molding Minds, Recruiting Bodies

How War Uses Public Relations and Propaganda

The people can always be brought to the bidding of the leaders. That is easy. All you have to do is tell them they are being attacked and denounce the pacifists for lack of patriotism and exposing the country to danger. It works the same way in any country.
—Hermann Goering, German Nazi Party leader

Propaganda: *Any form of communication in support of national objectives designed to influence the opinions, emotions, attitudes, or behavior of any group in order to benefit the sponsor, either directly or indirectly.*
—Department of Defense Dictionary of Military and Associated Terms

What do Marlboro cigarettes, the German Nazi Party, military recruiters, and Kellogg's Frosted Flakes cereal have in common? They all employ the same public-relation techniques to persuade people to think in a certain way and to want a certain thing.

One of the main problems governments face in waging war is getting soldiers to kill and die in them. War and military recruitment for war have always acted to manufacture the consent of the public. The military often calls propaganda—used against the populations of adversary governments, neutral allies, or the United States population—"information war" or "psychological operations." Today hundreds of millions of dollars fund private and government research, analysis, public relations, and advertising to up recruitment numbers. A good deal of the military's recruitment budget of $3.9 billion is spent on slick ads that reach students before they set foot on campus—in fashion and music magazines, free iPod downloads, MySpace campaigns, on television and hip-hop radio stations, and through concert and sporting event sponsorships.[75] If we want to counter the recruitment of youth for war or the manipulation of the public to support war, we must understand how propaganda is used by the military.

Modern public relations and propaganda were born during the First World War to convince Americans to go to war. President Woodrow Wilson formed the Committee for Public Information and appointed Walter Lippmann and psychologist Edward Bernays. Within six months the group had generated a propaganda campaign that successfully dehumanized Germans and created anti-German hysteria, so that Americans would be more supportive of fighting a war against them. This was at a time when trade unionists, radicals, socialists, anarchists, and pacifists actively opposed fighting a war in which the working class of each country would be sent to kill the working class of the other for the benefit of those on top.

The "Father of public relations," a nephew of Sigmund Freud, Bernays pioneered the use of psychology in public persuasion, or what he called "engineering consent." After the First World War he went to work for big business, including Procter & Gamble, CBS, the American Tobacco Company, General Electric, and Dodge Motors. His book, *Crystallizing Public Opinion* was used by the Nazi propagandist Goebbels to consolidate Nazi power and win support for the campaign for the internment of Jews, Roma (Gypsies), dissidents, homosexuals, and other undesirables. Bernays said of his work, "If we understand the mechanism and motives of the group mind, it is now possible to control and regiment the masses according to our will without their knowing it."[76]

This thought was reflected when German politician, military, and Nazi Party leader Hermann Goering bluntly explained to the United States Army Intelligence officer Gustave Gilbert during the 1946 Nuremberg Nazi war-crimes trials, "Why, of course, the *people* don't want war. Why would some poor slob on a farm want to risk his life in a war when the best that he can get out of it is to come back to his farm in one piece? Naturally, the common people don't want war; neither in Russia nor in England nor in America, nor for that matter in Germany. That is understood. But, after all, it is the *leaders* of the country who determine the policy and it is always a simple matter to drag the people along, whether it is a democracy or a fascist dictatorship or a Parliament or a Communist dictatorship."[77]

Walter Lippmann, a well-known journalist and co-founder of the *New Republic* magazine, also worked on the Committee for Public Information and later went on to join President Wilson's administration as Assistant to the Secretary of War. Lippmann coined the term "manufacturing consent" about which he said, "The creation of consent is not a new art. It is a very old one, which was supposed to have died out with the appearance of democracy. But it has not died out. It has, in fact, improved enormously in technic, because it is now based on analysis rather than on rule of thumb."

Recruitment Research

The first step for the military is to figure out why people do or do not join. Public and private research and analysis institutions spend millions of dollars every year to research, analyze, and then design policies and advertising campaigns to both recruit adequate numbers of military personnel and garner public support for government war and foreign policy. Some of the research specifically targets groups of potential recruits, like Latinos or those with high-tech skill. There is also a whole section of research, analysis, PR, and advertising aimed at "influencers"—those who influence young people's decisions like parents, teachers, counselors, priests, coaches, and the like.

Another more disturbing layer of research analyzes what they call "propensed" and "nonpropensed" youth, meaning those more or less likely to join the military. It is in these studies that they attempt to understand the psychological and subconscious beliefs and influences that shape the potential recruits' thinking and increase their propensity to join the military.

A 2005 study by the Joint Advertising Market Research and Studies (JAMRS) called *Military Knowledge Study: Measuring Military Knowledge and Examining its Relationship with Youth Propensity* has this to say:

> Propensed youth associated different images with the military than non-propensed youth. Of note, propensed youth associated both positive and negative concepts with war, whereas nonpropensed youth associated only negative concepts. Furthermore, propensed youth made a connection between war and personally relevant concepts, most importantly defending and protecting their family. The findings have direct implications for messages and images that can be used by recruiters and advertisers to more effectively target youth.
>
> While non-propensed youth may see the military as honorable and their family as honorable, this connection is not enough to motivate them toward

Camera Operator: SSGT. ARNOLD W. KALMANSON

> enlistment. Based on these results, the following recommendation is offered: Advertising messages that directly address issues of armed conflict are necessary. They must clearly communicate to youth the role of military service in defending and protecting their loved ones.

Another distinction between propensed and non-propensed youth was how they related rigidity to the military. Non-propensed youth made a direct connection between rigidity and the military, indicating an overall impression of the military as a rigid organization. On the other hand, propensed youth, similar to enlistees and recruiters, associated rigidity with specific aspects of the military. Propensed youth and recruiters associated rigidity with war, while enlistees associated rigidity with physical challenge. Based on these results, the following recommendation is offered: Advertising messages should emphasize flexible aspects of military life. They should also aim to 'contain' images of rigidity so that they are only associated with specific aspects of military service.

Yet another difference between propensed and non-propensed youth had to do with higher education. Higher education was a central concept for non-propensed youth, but not for propensed youth. The centrality of higher education, along with the fact that it was directly linked to obligation by non-propensed youth, indicates that higher education is very important to this group. While higher education was obviously important to non-propensed youth, they did not associate it with the military.

Based on these results, the following recommendation is offered: Advertising messages need to show non-propensed youth how they can serve in the Military and still fulfill their obligation to higher education. This is different from advertising money for college.[78]

Public Relations and Recruitment

After research and analysis, propagandists use branding and psychological manipulation techniques to help sustain the armed forces. Near the end of the Vietnam War in 1973 President Richard Nixon discontinued the draft and created the all-volunteer military. The draft had been massively unpopular and widely resisted. The military hired public relations and advertising firms to persuade youth to enlist, adopting recruiting messages to encourage enlistment.

The public relations industry web site Brandchannel.com describes branding as "a collection of perceptions in the mind of the consumer." A brand is very different from a product or service. The Army and other military branches have had many slogans that help fashion their brand. "Be All You Can Be," for example, was named the second most popular advertising jingle of the last century by *Advertising Age* magazine.

Air Force Organizational Emblem: Information Warfare Battlelab, Air Intelligence Agency. Camera Operator: AF HISTORICAL RESEARCH AGENCY, 1997

Army Recruitment Slogans:

"I want YOU for the US Army"
First and Second World Wars

"Today's Army wants to join you"
1971–73

"Join the people who've joined the Army"
1973–1979

"This is the Army"
1979–1981

"Be all you can be"
1981–2001

"An Army of one"
2001–2006

"Army strong"
2006–?

Other Branches of the Military Slogans:

"Army National Guard: You Can"
Army National Guard

"Aim high"
Air Force

"Do something amazing"
Air Force

"Accelerate your life"
Navy

"The Few, The Proud, The Marines"
Marines

Army of One

Good advertising does not just circulate information. It penetrates the public mind with desires and belief.
—Leo Burnett

By the end of the 1990s recruitment was down and "Be All You Can Be" was no longer working. "Kids don't like it," said Ray DeThorne of Leo Burnett, the ad agency that took over PR for the Army and produced the "Army of One" campaign "They say it's the voice of their parents telling them what to do."[79]

In an online open discussion of the "U.S. Army brand" on Brandchannel.com, one industry professional wrote, "The brand value of the U.S. Army is taking a body blow: customers (recruits) are staying away; shareholders (U.S. citizens) have lost confidence in the CEO (Bush) to lead; and the product is, in fact, dangerous—see the recently leaked Pentagon report claiming that up to 80% of U.S. fatalities in Iraq could have been prevented by proper body armor. If the U.S. Army were a consumer product, the company would now be facing massive product-liability lawsuits."

During the periodic drops in recruitment the research-and-analysis machine kicks into high gear, recommending more recruiters, new PR and advertising approaches, increased pay, benefits, bonuses, and promises. Often the military hires new PR and advertising corporations to make over their recruitment image and branding. Leo Burnett Worldwide took the major PR and advertising contract after recruitment fell short in 1999.

Leo Burnett and his advertising agency are responsible for such advertising icons as the Marlboro Man, the Jolly Green Giant, the Pillsbury Doughboy, and Tony the Tiger. *Time* magazine called him the "Sultan of Sell," naming him one of the 100 most important people of the twentieth

century—the man most responsible for the blizzard of commercial images that assaults us everyday. Though an advertising message might be rejected consciously, he maintained that it was accepted subliminally. Through the "thought force" of symbols, he said, "we absorb it through our pores, without knowing we do so."[80]

In the first "Army of One" TV ad, a soldier is seen running alone through a vast desert. "I am an army of one," he says. "Even though there are 1,045,690 soldiers just like me, I am my own force. The might of the U.S. Army doesn't lie in numbers, it lies in me."

Louis Caldera, Secretary of the Army, says of young people, "What we are telling them is that the strength of the Army is in individuals. Yes, you're a member of the team and you've got support from your fellow teammates, but you as an individual make a difference."[81] Bob Garfield, an ad critic for *Advertising Age*, has a different view: "It's a clever campaign, but substantially dishonest. The Army is not, never has been, and never will be about one soldier. Individuality has absolutely nothing to do with Army life."[83]

Branding of the Future

In 2005 widespread counterrecruiting efforts culminated in disapproving public opinion to create a recruiting crisis, with many services failing to reach their quotas. In response the Army picked a new advertising agency, McCann Erickson Worldwide, which counts among its clients Coca-Cola, MasterCard, Maybelline, Microsoft, Johnson & Johnson, and Black & Decker. The agency was hired to help enhance the Army's communications with young people and their parents with a new campaign and slogan. *Advertising Age* ranked McCann as the #2 agency network worldwide in 2005, with revenues of $1.5 billion. Its web site boasts of its trademarked "McCann Brand Chain," which talks about "leveraging brand assets" to "create demand" for the agency's clients' products or services.

Army Strong

"There's strong, and then there's Army Strong," says the 30-second TV commercial. The screen fills with images of soldiers with guns running in shorts and Army t-shirts, saluting, boarding combat helicopters, and helping each other over training courses obstacles. Dramatic music plays and a voiceover says:

> It's more than physical strength; it is emotional strength. Not just strength in numbers, but strength of brothers. Not just the strength to get yourself over, the strength to get over yourself. There's nothing stronger than the U.S. Army, because there is nothing stronger than a U.S. Army soldier. There's strong, and then there's Army Strong.

In October 2006 the U.S. Army announced their new branding message. They sent out press releases and distributed copies of a three-minute "ethos" video to bloggers and YouTube. On November 11th—Veteran's Day—they began airing TV commercials with their new advertising slogan and brand identity. With a budget estimated at $1.35 billion over the next five years, Army Strong advertising will appear in conventional media like television and print ads as well as non-conventional outlets like blogs, MySpace, other social networking web sites, and chat rooms.

"Army Strong" is the U.S. Army's effort to re-brand itself, putting into practice cutting-edge research, analysis, and propaganda techniques in an effort to shape the minds and decisions of young people, their parents, and their communities.

Stuart Elliott of the *New York Times* wrote of the ad campaign, "A prized goal of Madison Avenue is to link a brand to a desirable quality or attribute: Ford trucks with toughness, Coca-Cola with refreshment, FedEx with reliability. Now comes a major effort from one of the oldest brands of all, the Army, to lay claim to the concept of strength."[83]

To give the ads popular appeal, the Army hired award-winning music video director Samuel Bayer to direct the

ARMY ST

ONG.
U.S

commercials. Bayer launched his career in 1991 with the music video for Nirvana's "Smells Like Teen Spirit," which MTV has recognized as one the most influential music videos ever made. Since then, Bayer has directed music videos for the Rolling Stones, Marilyn Manson, Metallica, the Smashing Pumpkins, David Bowie, Aerosmith, Lenny Kravitz, Blink-182, and Green Day. His advertising work includes campaigns for Nike, Coca-Cola, Pepsi, Nissan, Lexus, and Mountain Dew.

Lieutenant General Robert L. Van Antwerp oversees recruiting as Commanding General of the Army Accessions Command. In an Army public relations news interview he was asked what message "Army Strong" will send to potential recruits. He responded, "We tested it with twenty-six different focus groups. They want to go to that next step in their life. Wherever they are. And the Army is going to help them get there. That's the whole point. That's what the Army does for me. It makes me stronger than when I came in."[84]

As noted earlier, the 2005 study of recruitment-age youth showed that propensed youth draw a connection between the military and their families. "Army Strong" ads target these youth by clearly connecting the military to approval and respect from families through images and words.

In several "Army Strong" TV commercials, the Army uses real soldiers and their families, including a Latino family and a young African American man and his family. In another, we are introduced to a young white soldier named Brandon Talsma and his parents on their farm in Monroe, Iowa. Brandon says, "It was tough to tell them I was joining the Army at first—and not because of the obstacle course." His father responds, "I'm pretty nervous, uh, apprehensive, but I'm very proud of him." His mother adds, "He's just a stronger, more driven individual." In this way, the ads also target "influencers" like parents, teachers, and other adults by using positive images of soldiers. Another commercial ends with a voiceover saying, "If your son or daughter wants to talk about the Army, listen. You made them strong, we'll make them Army Strong."

This concept of "strong" is not without problems. A comment posted on the blog Norwegianity.com explains, "I think this ad is for the folks at home who desperately want their kids who are serving to come back as better people, and not as broken-down fucked-up pieces of bio-hazardous waste."[85]

National Public Radio radio host Bob Garfield writes on the website AdAge.com: "Iraq is a tough sell. The recruiting command has met its targets only by lowering standards on education levels and basic aptitude. What it doesn't do is acknowledge the elephant in the room. Save for one flashing image in the sixty seconds of a medic placing his stethoscope to the chest of a healthy-looking Iraqi boy, there is not the slightest reference to wartime. The strength message scans as far as it goes, but is drowned out by the deafening silence about violent reality."[86]

A group called Texans for Peace put up a web site challenging the "Army Strong" campaign called ArmyWrong.net. Their mission reads, "Army Wrong is a new front in an escalating insurgency to counter the $200 million per year the Army spends on campaigns squarely aimed at the youth of America—packed with images of power and hyped across the full media spectrum. Counterrecruiting efforts like Army Wrong are hoping to do something more serious . . . obstruct the creeping militarism of America and war policies by encouraging youth to find other forms of service."

The site features commentary, recruitment and counter recruitment-related news, and realistic images of soldiers at war, as well as the "Army Wrong" take on the new advertising slogan: "There's wrong and then there's Army

Wrong. The courage to resist today. The courage to resist tomorrow. There is nothing on this green earth that is stronger than integrity."[87]

Research of Public Support for War

Just as research and analysis is done to understand and increase military recruitment, it is also done to understand public support for military operations and wars. The United States military–directed study by the Rand Institute, *American Public Support for U.S. Military Operations from Mogadishu to Baghdad,* explains the "the key factors that are associated with—and can be used to predict—support or opposition for military operations."

These factors are:

- Importance of the stakes. Beliefs about the importance of the United States' stakes in a situation are associated with support and opposition for military operations there—whether in terms of vital national interests, security interests, or moral or humanitarian interests.
- Prospects for success. Beliefs about the prospects for a successful outcome in the operation are with support or opposition.
- Expected and actual casualties and other costs. Beliefs about the likely costs, especially in casualties, are also associated with support.
- Partisan leadership and "followership." These beliefs, and support and opposition as well, are in turn related to partisan leadership and what we call "followership"—the inclination to follow one's party or ideological leaders.

The study notes that while public opinion is not the main factor in deciding on military operations, "public opinion shapes the way military operations are justified and in some cases conducted."

In the Iraq war, the report notes that, "The prevalence of beliefs about the importance of the stakes and, to a lesser extent, the high probability of success were the key sources that buoyed support; as a result, although casualty expectations were much higher than in the peace operations we examined, the willingness to tolerate casualties in a war in Iraq also was much higher."[88]

The Bush administration has used public relations and propaganda techniques more brazenly than any other administration in recent history in an effort to influence the "key factors" and mold public support for the wars in Iraq and Afghanistan and efforts to dominate Iran, North Korea, and Venezuela, and the underlying policies of empire. This has included "big lie" tactics of repetitive misinformation, such as linking Iraq with the September 11th attacks and claims of Iraqi stockpiles of nuclear weapons; fabricated news stories, such as the toppling of Saddam's statue just after the invasion of Iraq or the "rescue" of a United States servicewoman in Iraq, Jessica Lynch; hiring PR firms, creating newspapers in Iraq, planting false or misleading stories, and creating the Iraqi national Congress which pushed for a U.S. invasion; influencing the media through embedded reporting, control of information and access in Iraq, etc. The Bush administration has also created "memes" and stories to brand its foreign policies, like the "war on terror," "weapons of mass destruction," and "Operation Iraqi Freedom" (originally "Operation Iraqi Liberation," until people realized that the acronym spelled O-I-L).

Counterpropaganda

Understanding how advertising, public relations, and propaganda techniques are used to influence youth into enlisting and the public into supporting war and empire is essential to stopping predatory recruiting and illegal and immoral wars and occupations. Here are some ways we can counter this propaganda.

Leo Burnett Campaign

One approach to countering recruitment propaganda is to directly confront and pressure those that do the dirty propaganda work for the military. Students and youth in Chicago from Students for Justice, decided to confront the advertising firm that made the United States military's recruitment propaganda. Author/activist Naomi Klein wrote in early 2003, "In Chicago last week, more than a hundred high-school students demonstrated outside the headquarters of Leo Burnett, the advertising firm that designed the U.S. military's hip, youth-targeted 'Army of One' campaign. The students claim that in under-funded Latino and African American high schools, the army recruiters far outnumber the college scouts."[89]

Joe, an organizer with Students for Justice, explains their actions, which led to the arrests of a number of students: "The protests against Leo Burnett from Dec. '02 to April '03 exposed their role in this recruitment. They could not ignore the attention brought on them. No company wants negative publicity, especially a firm in an industry based on public opinion, like advertising."[90] The Chicago Business newspaper *Crains* revealed that the protests caused conflicts within the company. Some employees opposed the war and the Army of One contract.

Battle of the Story

One term that is helpful in understanding advertising, propaganda, and how to counter them is the concept of a "meme." Organizer and author Doyle Canning defines a "meme" as a unit of self-replicating cultural information—a slogan, melody, image or idea that bounces through the culture. Doyle is part of a group of organizers, trainers, strategists, and communications professionals called smart-Meme who have developed tools and who lead training for activists and communities to understand how we are manipulated by the stories and propaganda of those in power and how we might wage a "battle of the story," in which we powerfully communicate our own stories to counter theirs.

There are two kinds of memes. Another smartMeme organizer, Patrick Reinsborough, defines them:

controlMeme: a meme used to marginalize, coopt or limit the scale of social change ideas by institutionalizing a status-quo bias into popular perception of events. The type of memes that analysts from the United States military and government analysis and research think tank, RAND Corporation, and Pentagon information warfare experts spend countless hours and millions of dollars designing.

smartMeme: a designer meme, which injects new infectious ideas into popular culture, contests established meaning (controlMemes), and facilitates popular rethinking of assumptions. These are memes that act as containers for collaborative power, reveal creative possibilities for change, and help grassroots social movements contest idea space.

In section three of this book there is a "Battle of the Story" worksheet that can be used by individuals and groups to help them to understand the status-quo story on an issue, so that we can better tell our own counterstory.

At the core, much of what their advertising, branding, and PR does is to tell a story that influences our beliefs and thinking. Being able to understand, break down, and expose their stories and propaganda is key, but it's not enough to win. We also have to be able to tell and amplify our own real-life stories clearly, powerfully, and effectively.

SECTION TWO

COUNTER-RECRUITMENT

DON'T
ENLIST
FOR WAR AND
TORTURE

COUNTERRECRUIT TO WIN

I have three daughters who are targets for the military, so it became clear . . . that one of the most practical things we could do was to counter military recruitment in the high schools. It's embarrassing what the military does—driving humvees onto campus, landing helicopters in middle schools, getting pretty girls to come out and get people's addresses, offering lottery drawings for cars in exchange for the student's name and address.
—Chris Venn, parent activist[91]

Getting the military out of our schools and replacing them with real educational opportunities is our generation's fight. No one will do it for us. We owe it to ourselves, the Iraqis, and the American soldiers dying for a lie.
—Student comment posted on Jorge Mariscal blog[92]

There's an art and science to effective counterrecruitment. The art is in the relationships you build in the school and larger community—with students, vets, teachers, and other organizations. The science is the mindful way you plan activities in the school and community according to the unique situation of a particular school. Both are needed to make your work effective. According to the leading experts in counterrecruitment, there are common characteristics of successful counterrecruitment.

Although you may start without all these components in place, your long-term strategy should make sure that your efforts:

Support youth activists and activism. The best counterrecruiters are fellow students. Students need material support and community resources to be successful. In addition, organizers must appreciate the value of youth activism in the transformation of society and schools.

Approach teachers and other school personnel as potential allies. Don't assume school personnel want to keep counterrecruiters out. Take the path of least resistance when working in a new school. Identify friendly teachers—through word of mouth and antiwar events—who will invite counterrecruitment presentations in class. Ask for referrals to other teachers and other schools. First create a track record of work with students before approaching the administration with policy or rule changes. When talking to school employees, give recognition to the challenges they face in providing educational services to young people. Minimize confrontational language and avoid making them feel harassed by establishing friendly, informal relationships as much as possible.

Bring veterans to the forefront. The experience of those who have been recruited and served reaches students effectively. Find vets by contacting a local Veterans for Peace chapter or the national office of Iraq Veterans Against the War. Both organizations keep a list of veterans interested in classroom presentations by region. The Committee Opposed to the Militarism of Schools in San Diego County found many veterans by running a simple ad in the free weekly: "Antiwar veterans sought for high school presentations."

Have a well-thought-out message. Consider how your message can help or hinder your equal access efforts. A message that articulates values everyone can agree on gets the most mileage. For example, you may want to discuss "honest recruiting," "teaching nonviolence, " or "providing concrete career and community service opportunities to youth." You may win people over who otherwise would be resistant to open criticism of the war. Check out the mission of Nonmilitary Options for Youth (NOY), an Austin, Texas, group comprised of veterans, parents, activists, students, and others who formed the group in 1997. They write, "Believing in nonviolence, we seek to balance the military recruiting information given in the high schools and explore with students the many alternate choices available to them."[93]

Approach organizing in a collaborative and flexible way. Work in coalition with community groups and/or solicit key endorsements. Make sure your effort represents, or at least speaks to the concerns of, diverse constituencies (that is, people of color, women, those with low incomes). Include veterans in your leadership and your pool of educational-resource people. Plan to bring forward letters, emails, and phone calls of complaint about the military from parents, students, community groups, and school personnel. They are very effective.

- Explore if the teachers' union can be an ally. Some states have Educators Against War groups. In one Chicago school district, which has the highest percentage of military academies, teachers are leading the fight to demilitarize schools.
- Contact local antiwar groups to see if they have contacts with students, teachers, or vets.
- Build a diverse and sophisticated network with other campaigns. For example, you can reach out to labor or immigrant rights organizations. When Fernando Suarez de Solar, an immigrant from Mexico, lost his son in the

Iraq War, he drew on ties to both the peace and immigrant rights movements in the spring of 2006 to organize a historic 231-mile march from Tijuana to San Francisco to bring a message of peace to immigrant youth heavily targeted by recruiters.

Systematically build over time. The CAMS Adopt A School approach begins with an assessment at the school and district level and then creates short- and long-term plans, and measures results. Many counterrecruitment efforts begin with fliering and outreach to classrooms at a specific school. They later move on to career centers and fairs, to challenging the ASVAB tests on campus, to supporting student peace clubs, and eventually district-wide changes in the student data reporting and rules governing military access to students.

Support your equal access rights. Know your legal rights as a student, parent, teacher, or community member. Insist that counterrecruiters have the same access to school and students as do military recruiters. Counterrecruiters have effectively argued for clarification or changes in school district policy to stop the military from having privileged access. The Ninth Circuit Court of Appeals decision, *San Diego Committee v. Governing Bd.*, 790 F.2d 1471 (9th Cir. 1986) No. 83-6070, states that the question of military service (whether voluntary or compulsory) is a controversial political (not economic or academic) issue, and if a school establishes a forum for one side to present its views on the issue, it must give opponents equal access to the forum.

Have materials in Spanish or other relevant languages. Many of the youth targeted for recruitment speak a language other than English in their homes. Assess

Graphic courtesy of Committee Opposed to Militarism and the Draft

the need for material in Spanish or other relevant languages. The Latino population is key to the Pentagon meeting its recruitment numbers—the military acknowledges Latinos as a fast-growing population underrepresented in the military ranks. The Committee Opposed to Militarism and the Draft in San Diego offers brochures in Spanish.[94] Code Pink San Francisco has developed counterrecruitment material in Chinese.

Create a centralized place for information and contact. You can create a simple web site to answer questions, to distribute material, to allow parents and students to report concerns, and to collect data.

Have a clear understanding of the place military recruitment plays in the antiwar movement. As discussed earlier, counterrecruitment is an essential part of a larger strategy to change the world we live in. It is important to appreciate the work you do within this context and share this larger vision with all those you impact.

Students protesting militarism at their high school.
Photo courtesy CAMS.

YOUR BLOOD
FOR OUR PROFITS!
Thanks!
From your friends at...
HALLIBURTON
oldamericancentury.org

KNOW YOUR RIGHTS: Equal Access in Public Schools

In the last dozen years, military training programs in high schools have approximately doubled. Now, half a million secondary students are attending Junior ROTC classes daily, and militaristic programs like the Young Marines are springing up in middle schools. Tanks and helicopters are being brought into elementary schools for children to play in, and a growing network of official partnerships between military units and K-12 schools is making field trips to military bases a routine occurrence in some communities.
—Rick Janhkow[95]

First things first. In order to effectively counterrecruit, you should learn and defend your rights. Some groups have created fliers with the following information, and they send out volunteers armed with this information.

As a private citizen:

- You have a right to hand out materials to students before they enter school grounds, but you cannot enter school grounds without permission (boundaries may extend beyond the building).
- You have a right to have a table in a park that has only printed materials.
- You have a right to march on a public sidewalk.

Check local rules to determine if local permits are required to:

- March in the street.
- Stage a rally of more than twenty people.
- Use a bullhorn or other source of amplified sound.

Contact local groups to learn from their past experience with local law enforcement

As a student:

- You have a right to organize, promote, and participate in organizations and political groups.
- You have a right to circulate newspapers, literature, or political leaflets on school property.
- You have a right to wear political or other types of buttons, badges, or armbands and to post bulletin-board notices within the schools.

You have a right to express your opinions, but schools can set restrictions on when, where, and how. Schools may require review and prior consent of materials to be distributed. This review must be completed in a brief and definite period, and there must be standard criteria for approval or rejection. Schools can forbid distribution of obscene or libelous material and prohibit blocking hallways and entrances.

Schools are bound to respect the law of equal access. If a school allows military recruiters, it cannot keep out organizations offering information about jobs in the peace movement. If the school, district or city denies your right to freedom of expression, contact the ACLU at www.aclu.org to find a local office or affiliate. There are school districts that have clarified their equal-access policy by writing a letter to school sites. Organizers can carry these letters in case they are questioned about counterrecruitment activities.

When the military comes to your local high school, you have a legal right to give students an opposing view. The strongest support for this right comes from a Ninth Circuit Court ruling on equal access, which states that the government-sponsored forums must allow both sides of "controversial and political" subjects, like the question of military service (whether voluntary or compulsory). Counterrecruiters can reference this decision as a lever to get schools to cooperate, and as a way to assuage concerns of teachers, counselors, and school administrators nervous about having counterrecruiters on campus. An excellent in-depth explanation of equal-access law and how it was used in a large school system can be found on Project YANO's web site at www.projectyano.org/pdf/Equalaccess2006.pdf.

Pursuing new lawsuits is no small effort and could potentially drain resources from essential student outreach activities. If necessary, work with legal experts to use the Ninth Circuit equal-access and similar rulings to gain entrance into your local schools.[96]

Graphic: Andy Menconi, www.notyoursoldier.org

TACTICS ON CAMPUS
Mass Distribution: Into the Students' Hands

Fliering

Use up-to-date materials. This is important. Make sure that the fliers and data you use are recent so that your efforts are based on the current wartime situation.

Luckily, the easiest counterrecruitment activity to organize is one of the most effective. Personal outreach through leafleting at schools is directly influential, especially when students are involved.

In 2005 a coalition of peace groups decided that they would leaflet at twenty-three of San Diego County's high schools. Rick Jahnkow of Project YANO remembers, "We would choose a morning, preferably Fridays, to hand out up-to-date literature and facts about recruiting. Sometimes it was the opt out information, sometimes it was the 'Ten Things You Should Know' flier. We found that these leaflets found their way into the classrooms that day and often would be the subject of conversation that day. In fact, teachers and students would sometimes come back out and ask us for a stack of fliers to share with the class. This was a great

Students at Vista High School distribute flyers to fellow students before school. Photo: Rick Jahnkow, Committee Opposed to Militarism and the Draft.

way to hook up with student activists, too. They would find us and begin to hand out fliers themselves. By the end of the year, our coalition had distributed thousands of fliers, and about thirty percent of fliers were passed out by the students themselves."[97]

Don't limit yourself to fliering at the school site. If you have a hard time getting access to campus, or just want to reach more kids, look beyond the campus. California State Los Angeles student Manual Derate found a local coffeehouse where high school students hung out. This became his counterrecruitment station. He passed out information and talked to people. Every school has a hangout—is there a packed burger or juice joint nearby?

Tabling

Counterrecruiters can establish a good presence at school events by tabling. Set up a portable table, put out literature, make an appealing display, and then use it to reach out to students and hand them literature. If recruiters are setting up a table at a school event, from a football game to Mexican Heritage Month, then you have a legal right to set up a table, too. Contact the event organizers at school, often an administrator or counselor, to make arrangements.

Susan Van Haitsma with Nonmilitary Options for Youth in Austin, Texas, shares her secret to tabling success, "We began by approaching contacts we had in the schools and asking to have literature tables during career fairs and looking for opportunities to do classroom presentations. We started increasing the number of things we gave away—starting with buttons and adding edibles such as 'peace

Students distributing counter recruitment materials and info at lunchtime on campus. Photo courtesy CAMS

cookies.' At first our cookies were homemade sugar cookies with peace signs on them. They were pretty popular, but also labor intensive! Then we hit upon the idea of giving away fortune cookies, which are reasonably priced in bulk and which carry on the theme of 'your future.' We decided to give away 'conscientious objector' buttons as an educational tool. We ask students who take them if they know what the term means. The buttons open an avenue for information sharing about a concept with which most students are unfamiliar. We also began giving away copies of the book *Addicted to War* in English and Spanish. One of the veterans in our group donated a box for us to use one year, and we found the books to be a valuable and popular resource. Now, we budget enough to give away about ten books per school every semester. Several of the high-school libraries also have the book. Sometimes librarians are our best allies."[98]

Non military career options literature on display.
Photo courtesy COMDSD.

Career Days

We know the military recruiters will be back to Garfield High, but so will we.

—Arlene Inuoye, Committee Against the Militarization of Schools

In May 2005, Military Day at Garfield High School had tables and tables of military recruiters from all branches of the military giving out free branded items like water bottles, calendars, langards, and visors to any student who was a willing taker—with just their name, phone number, and contact information in exchange. Students eagerly signed up to try the pull-up bars and take the free merchandise. One of the largest in the country, Garfield High School is an overcrowded school with over 95 percent students of Latino heritage in a working-poor community in East Los Angeles. In 2004 it ranked fifth in the nation for having the

Career center display in a high school.
Photo courtesy Project on Youth and Non-Military Options.

largest number of Hispanics recruited with signed contracts for the United States army.

Fast forward to Military Day in May 2006. This year the Committee Against the Militarization of Our Schools (CAMS) Adopt A School Project, which mobilizes teams of counterrecruiters at individual schools, was initiated at Garfield. By gathering data regarding the military recruitment at the school and then employing case-specific strategies, a plan of action was developed.

One was to subvert the Military Day by providing the real information about the enlistment contract and details on how to file as a conscientious objector. The counter-recruiter team at Garfield consisted of students from MEChA, Inner City Struggle youth, the social justice academy learning community and its twelve teachers, a team of neighbouring California State University social work students, and an ELA Community college recruiter.

The group met in the lunch quad on a warm spring day. Several festively displayed tables were filled with information about college, literature on the truth about enlisting, surveys requesting the students' opinions about the war in Iraq, along with "I Will Not Kill" statements and cards to sign and file. Most noticeable were over a dozen people with hand-painted t-shirts and signs with their own slogans, ("Books Not Bombs," "Out of Iraq," "Proud 2 be Antiwar," "School=Success, War=Death," "Save Iraqi Children," "Recruit Bush, NOT my students," "Young people are the future but they are dying," "Education, Not Extermination") who paraded around the school, past the career center, where it was announced that two military recruiters, there to talk with interested students, sat alone and thumbed the newspaper. They later just took off.

Surveys and letters written by Garfield High students expressed deep concern about military recruitment, with a majority feeling that it is inappropriate for them to be on high-school campuses at all. Many have experienced the relentless intrusions of military recruitment in their lives. In 2006 the students reclaimed Military Day as *Military Free Day.*

It remains to be seen if Military Day will resurface in coming years. Counterrecruiters have to stay vigilant and the organizer networks strong in order to face future challenges.

Story: Peace Poetry Contest in Texas

In 2004 Nonmilitary Options for Youth sponsored a "peace poetry" contest for its twelve district high schools. The contest winner gave some great advice to counterrecruiters: "Don't just tell us what you think, ask us what we think!" The beauty of the poetry contest is that it honors an important principle in successful counterrecruitment—supporting student leadership and activism. A poetry contest (or an essay or a song writing contest) offers a stage to the contestants and encourages young people to consider and express their own opinions about the issue. It is a terrific way to build student voice—and in the end there is a real result on paper.

We've reprinted the winner of the 2004 contest below.

VOTE OR DIE

By Christopher Floyd

Junior, Reagan High School, Austin, TX

Born as a political activist / blessed with a wrath in my fist / strong enough to capture a glitch of the future after collapsing the bricks / It has been a tough road traveled on / too rough for the love boat / An ocean filled with blood from cutthroats / flowing through the aqueducts of

Babylon / trailed by tag-along soldiers who embrace war / face forward / toward death / is a sense a moving tongue has never tasted before / In time between time / demons speak the language of eternal fire in the form of politics just to weaken the mind / in the course of this presidential election / there has to be someone other than I stressing about this organic oppression which is the greatest depression / 1 step away from the edge of destruction / by the time we unfold the blindness from our hypocritical lenses / reconstruction will be worth nothing / to our sisters, brothers, mothers, fathers, aunts, uncles, grandmas, grandpas / and even the offspring of all my lost cousins will have to suffer in sorrow tomorrow for the vote of today / I'd speak my mind for youth but the choke in my throat STOPS the flow of truth / I guess I should speak for myself instead for you / since most minds of my kind are ignorant trifling / mainly concerned with the least important / EATING / SLEEPING / SNORING / and DRINKING / SMOKING / SNORTING / and their reason is life is too boring / Ha! If that's the case maybe we should say / FORGET IRAQ / turn our back / load our guns / hold our lungs from the pollution and label MURDER as our solution / since we abuse our own brain / what's the use then? / what's the use NOW? / what's the use of federal prisons within our government system when the owner doesn't listen / unless it has some initiative to do with trapping us in cell blocks / That's why I rather be pepper sprayed or shell shocked / any day / than to be caged in HELL hot as HELL 4-ever and more / having conversations with the devil like never before / the ghetto has drug galore / hysteria isn't cared for/ that's why Florida defeated Al Gore/ & Kerry is just another fish on the shore called the poll / Poverty is so poor / we can't even dis the rich no more / Is it because our souls are tired / or our voices are lazy / or our financial status is defaulting from all the choices we're making / This nation is BLIND with open eyes / Despite the draft / We're about to see the truth the meaning of "VOTE OR DIE!"

Student Survey

During the spring semester of 2006 students from Garfield High School held an opinion poll throughout the other eleven schools of their district, where students could vote to "Bring the Troops Home," "Keep Fighting in Iraq," or "Other: Your idea. What would you say to the President (respectfully, please)?" Students voted by placing colored stickers on poster boards with those choices. Organizers figured, how could the school district disapprove of an exercise that promoted democracy?

The vote totals ended with 100 for "Keep fighting in Iraq" and 703 for "Bring the Troops Home." There were also quite a few interesting responses on the "What would you say to the President?" poster, which the group then posted on its web site. Polls are a good way to open up spaces where kids can talk about these issues.

Classroom Presentations

Classrooms are an excellent place to open up discussions among students that may be sustained beyond your initial visit. Find sympathetic teachers willing to have you visit their class to discuss the military, war, and recruitment and schedule class periods to visit. One of the best things you can do as an organizer is train others how to present appropriately and effectively in a classroom. If possible, organize annual trainings. A sample outline with ideas on how to present follows.

Sample Outline for Classroom Presentation

The standard classroom presentation is usually done by two people—a vet and a community member—over a one-hour period. The community person begins with an icebreaker, describes the purpose of the visit, summarizes the agenda, gives a few disclaimers, and explains what motivates him or her to be there speaking with students. He or she then introduces the other speaker, a military veteran. The vet tells about his/her background and why he/she wants to speak to students, and then introduces the video. A common video is a clip from Michael Moore's documentary *Fahrenheit 9/11*. After the video, take questions or pose them to get a discussion going (which sometimes is the hardest part).

1. Get to Know the Students
   A. Ask for a show of hands:
      - How many of you have immediate family members who have been in the military? Which branches of the military?
      - Have any of you ever heard from a recruiter? Where/how?
      - How many of you have seen or heard military ads on TV or the radio, or seen them in magazines or newspapers?
      - Are any of you thinking of joining the military?

2. Our View and Our Purpose
   Say: We believe that the military is not for everyone. Some like it and make it their career, but some feel that joining was a big mistake. The problem is that it is a mistake you can't easily change, and one that does affect the rest of your life. With other kinds of jobs, if you don't like your work, you can quit and look for something else.

Gulf War veteran Eric Shaw (center) and Iraq War Vet Tina Garnarez (on right) with student moderator at a classroom counterrecruitment presentation, 2006. Photo: Alternatives to War through Education.

Peace Club members sharing information about militarism and recruitment. Photo courtesy CAMS.

Iraq-era Navy veteran and GI resister Pablo Paredes speaks to a high school class. Photo by Susan Quinlan, Alternatives to War through Education.

Pablo Paredes challenging a Navy recruiter at Kennedy High in Richmond, after speaking to students about his experiences in the military. Photo by Susan Quinlan, Alternatives to War Through Education.

But if you quit your job in the military, you can go to jail. We are here to help you learn more about the military than what is in all the commercials. We will let you know about other opportunities for job training and college money and careers in peacemaking and social change.

Say: We'll be presenting some of this information in our presentation and in a video we're going to show. We also have literature with information on job-training programs, college financial aid, and youth service projects.

With regard to the military, we're not going to give both sides. Why? Because young people are already constantly hearing why the military thinks they should join. Instead, we're going to give reasons why you might NOT want to go into the military, so you can put them together with the other things you've heard and get a more balanced picture.

We're not here to tell you what you should or shouldn't do regarding the military. We are going to give you our side on the issue, but what's most important to us is that you:

- Look for more information,
- Question everything you hear (including what we say), and
- Make up your own mind. It's not a decision that should be made by us, your parents, teachers, or anyone else, only you.

3. The speaker explains what motivates him/her to give up his/her time talking to students about these issues.

4. Introduce the veteran—the vet gives personal background, explains why he/she wants to talk to young people, uses personal anecdotes, and describes key lessons he/she learned about the military that young people should know.
5. The vet introduces the video—mention that afterwards time will be spent discussing any questions or comments the audience may have.
6. After the video draw attention to any literature available to pick up.

Suggested Questions for Class Discussion:

- What different ways can you serve your country?
- Are the country and the government the same thing?
- Is it our duty to serve our government, or is it our government's duty to serve us?
- Should one always obey all laws? If not, how does one decide when not to?
- What does "patriotism" mean to you?
- Can you be a strong, intelligent, and brave American and not support the military or United States military policy?
- Who decides when we should go to war?
- Under what circumstance would you be willing to go to war?
- Should one always follow orders? How do you decide?

—Adapted and excerpted from Project YANO and AWE's classroom guides.

OTHER TIPS TO STUDENT ACTIVISTS:

- Contact the student newspaper to place counterrecruitment ads.
- Build a group—welcome students who join tabling and fliering efforts at their school.
- Raise money or work with local jobs programs to create internships so that youth can get paid to do counterrecruitment work.
- Run a raffle. Collect student contact data and distribute counterrecruitment information, as well as information about community college, school grants, etc.

High School Soldiers

By Ryan Harvey

A child from my high school
Was sent off to Iraq
He got shot in the head
He's never coming back
I didn't really know him
But I know a lotta kids
Who sold themselves as soldiers
Whose fate may be like his

It makes me think of high school
And the kids who walked the halls
I wonder just how many
When off to heed the call
Who closed their eyes so quickly
And bought the myth of war
The promise of honor
Or a heart that beats no more

I think about the hallway
That was right outside the gym
I think about that doorway
With students coming in
Right by the cafeteria
Where lunch was everyday
Where the Army had their table
And gave free pens away
I saw those pens a lot
"Be All That You Can Be"
"Murder a couple families
And we'll pay for your degree"
They always mention money
As if soldiers come home rich!
They tricked you into killing
And you fell for it . . .

I remember many times
When I saw that table there
And I curse myself to think
That I never made it clear
That this is not normality
It's not another trend
It's soldiers in my hallway
Murdering my friends

Now I say it loudly
Wishing I was there
"Fuck you recruiters!
Stop targeting my peers!"
It's not my war to fight in
Neither is it yours
You're sending kids like me
To die in other people's wars

So stop and think my friends
Next time you see Marines
Talking to your classmates
Think just what it means

Cuz soldiers are not heroes
Let's make it clearly known
They're kids like you and
me
Whose hearts and minds
were overthrown

So don't be scared of
nothing
Please take my advice
If they start talking to your
classmates
Stand your ground and fight
And don't be fooled by
fables
That the textbook authors
type
Their wars are fought for
profit
Not for people's rights.

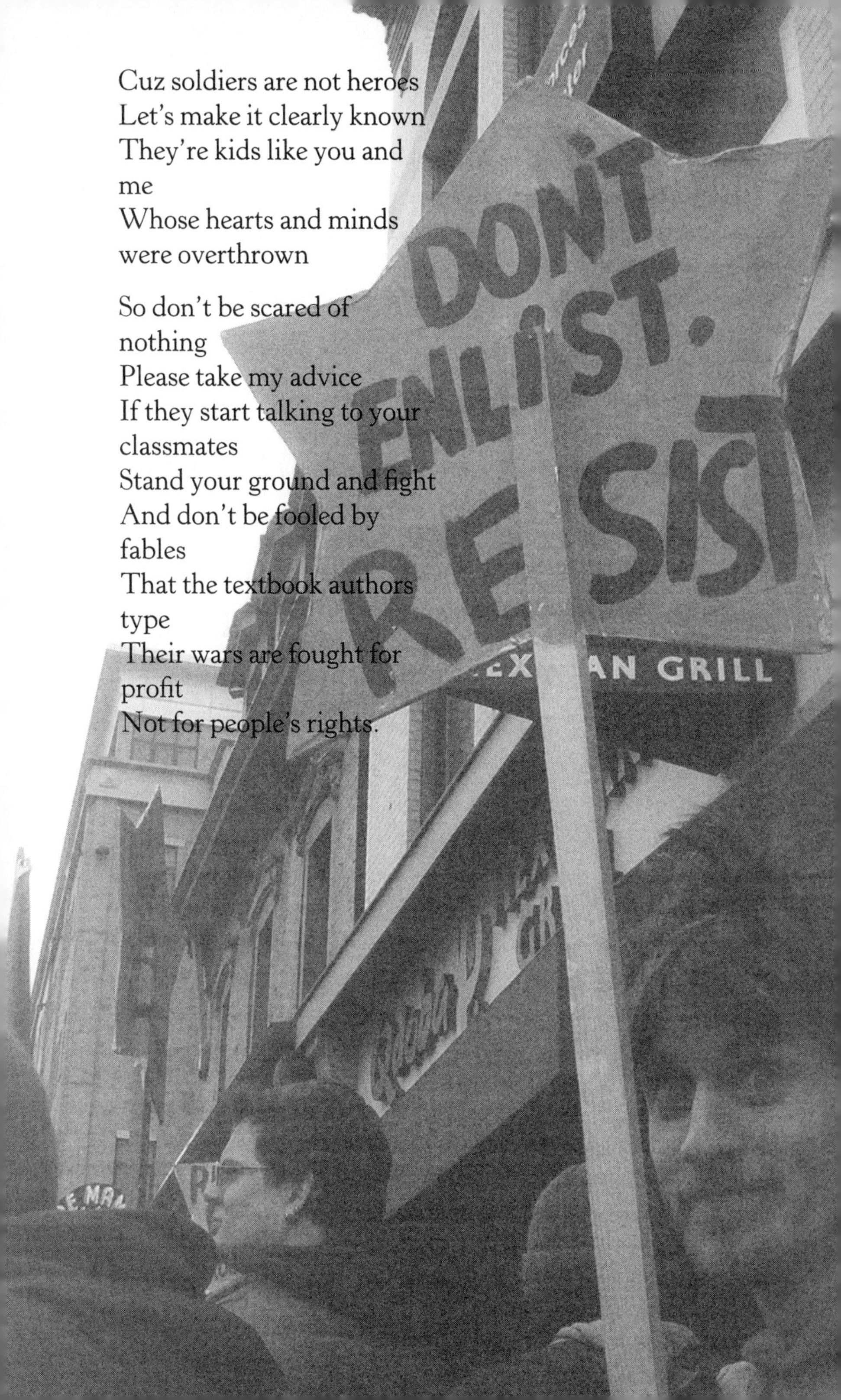

People are dying and the numbers keep on growing... Over 2,600 US troops have died in the last 3 years of war. Over 19,400 have been injured, many returning home disabled with everything from multiple missing limbs to severe psychological disorders. 5,500 US troops have gone AWOL since war began. US soldiers have killed anywhere from 30,000-100,000+ civilians and untold tens of thousands of enemy forces.

ARE YOU READY TO KILL? FOR A CAUSE YOU DON'T BELIEVE IN?

Taking a life is some heavy stuff. Killing someone is a decision you'll have to live with forever, and it's one you can't take back. Do you want to kill simply because you're ordered to do so? Or because conditions are so stressful you snap? Or make a rash split-second decision? Are you willing to bomb peoples' homes and destroy their livelihoods? Do you want to be under orders to fire on cars that don't realize they have to stop before reaching US checkpoints? Do you want to be one of the many soldiers returning home saying they killed innocent people because they had to, or they didn't know or made a mistake...

WHO CONTROLS YOUR LIFE?

Joining the military not only means you're legally obligated to do these things if ordered, it also means you'll be doing them with no control over why. Enlistment means giving up power and control over the most basic freedoms in life; what you eat, where you live, what you say, what you do after work, and more. It means simply that it isn't your life anymore.

FREEDOM OF CHOICE PUTS YOU IN CONTROL

Right now none of us would take a life just because someone we respected (parents, teacher, faith leader, principle, or friends) ordered us to, because we're independent thinkers. It's called freedom of choice and getting out of school and out on our own should mean we have even more of it, not less. Enlisting is like going back to grade school except you have a lot more teachers and a lot more things you have to do. Remember when your parents wanted you to do something and you wanted to know why? Or you didn't understand the point of it? Or you thought there was a better way to do it? The military means years of people yelling at you, "because I told you so."

DO YOU ALWAYS LISTEN TO WHAT COMMERCIALS TELL YOU?

Hell no. Then shouldn't you be skeptical of the claims recruiters make? They pretend to be a mentor, counselor, and coach-type figure, but in the end they exist solely to sell you the idea that it's for a cool, hip, and important future that you're signing away your life on the dotted line.

WHO'S LOOKING OUT FOR WHO?

Recruiters are **getting paid** to convince you to go risk your life for the decisions of rich politicians you probably didn't even vote to elect. They have a set quota of recruits they're required to "get" each month or they could get "reassigned" aka likely shipped off to Iraq. **1 in 5 recruiters is currently under investigation by the army** for things such as lying, cheating, deceiving and harassing recruits, sexual harassment, and other inappropriate behaviors, often engaged in for the purpose of meeting quotas. The cases are disturbing; recruiters tell people to lie about medical conditions that would disqualify them, recruiting a man fresh out of a 3-week stay in a psychiatric ward, etc. Lie on your enlistment and it's your butt that will be in trouble later, you're the one who'll be dishonorbably discharged. Agree to hide a medical condition and you're the one who could be injured or die later. The recruiters won't be around to live with the consequences so don't let them pretend they're doing you a favor now.

THE IMPORTANCE OF AGENDAS

Without knowing peoples' larger agendas, how can you make an informed decision about what they're telling you? And if they aren't coming clean about some things how you can you trust the rest of what they're telling you? As this pamphlet demonstrates there is a lot that recruiters aren't saying about the benefits and reality of enlistment and military life.

Counterrecruitment folding brochure spread — side 1
Created by the Pittsburgh Organizing Group

OUR GROUP'S AGENDA?

You might be sitting there thinking, but don't these kids have their own agenda? Of course we do. Basically, we don't support the war in Iraq, we don't want to see any more of our friends coerced or tricked into killing and being killed. On a larger scale we disagree with a lot of the government's current actions, and we try to work towards a world based on mutual aid, peace, voluntary association, and human solidarity. We're trying to be upfront about where we're coming from.

WHAT WE HOPE YOU GET OUT OF THIS

We realize this pamphlet is far too short to address all the relevant issues about enlistment and military recruitment. Our hope is that presenting you with alternative information (compared to what you're normally bombarded with) will encourage you to find out more and spur you to take action.

LINKS FOR MORE INFO

For more information on our efforts see www.organizepittsburgh.org - pog@mutualaid.org

News about CR: www.CounterRecruiter.net
Underground Alliance: www.militaryfreezone.org
Military Families Speak Out: www.mfso.org
GI Rights: http://girights.objector.org
GI Rights Hotline: 800-394-9544

Flyer written, designed, and printed by POG (Pittsburgh Organizing Group), a youth-led activist group

The Real Deal On Enlistment

What you need to know about military recruitment in your school

Across the country, military recruiters are desperate for warm bodies to fight and die in our overseas adventures. Three years of unpopular war has stressed the army to the breaking point. Community resistance to the human and material cost of war has decimated the number of those willing to sign-up and allow the Bush Administration to continue to project its power without pause.

The government is now hiring thousands of additional recruiters and spending hundreds of millions more to deceive, distort, coerce, and convince people into thinking enlistment is a good choice for their future.

This flyer is part of our response. It's about confronting the distortions and the misrepresentations made by recruiters and exposing the reality of military life for enlistees. It's also about what **you can do** to help stop recruiters in your town. Personal education is the key to this fight because each of us has a neighbor, friend, relative, or classmate currently being targeted by recruiters. The more you know, the more you can be a voice speaking out against the stream of misinformation they're being bombarded with.

WHAT THE MILITARY ISN'T TELLING YOU ABOUT ENLISTMENT

Where do you want your life to go? Right now most likely you're in one of three situations. You either think you know exactly what you want to do after you graduate and you have a plan to achieve it. Or, you think you know what you want to do, but aren't sure of how you can achieve it. Or, you have no clue what you're going to do and you're sick of everyone asking and/or telling you. Well, in all those cases you're probably sick of people asking/telling you, but no matter what your situation is, the military isn't a good choice for your future.

THE MYTH OF EASY MONEY FOR COLLEGE

You've probably heard the hype, $70,000 for college through the Army GI bill! Get your education paid for, etc. The truth is, the amounts aren't what they're made out to be, you probably won't get any money, and if you do it won't be free money because you'll have worked your butt off for it. Let's break down the military's exaggerations. Because of all the fine print requirements to receive college benefits, **only 35% of enlistees receive any GI bill funds for college — only 15% of enlistees ever receive a college degree**. The average participant actually receives less money than a student who simply receives a Pell Grant and a Stafford Loan. If you're part of the 25% of enlistees who get dishonorably discharged you get... nothing. If you're part of the 33% who leave the military early you get... nothing. If you later decide not to go to college you get... nothing. Oh yeah, you also have to pay a **$1,200** non-refundable deposit during your first year of service to even be eligible for the program, and that's money you won't get back if you end up... getting nothing.

TAKE A VACATION AROUND THE WORLD!

Join the Army, travel to exciting places, meet new and different people - and kill them.

The Army says that you will get to travel the world. Growing up in a small town can make that a big draw. For every kid who wants to stay rooted in their community, there's another who understandably wants to see a bit more of the world. Enlistment in the guard, reserves, or army certainly means you won't stay here for long, but are you sure that's a good thing? Iraq is a place with a lot of interesting people and places, but you won't be going there to sightsee. Maybe it'll be a cakewalk, but it could just as easily be you riding around wearing heavy armor during 110 degree summers waiting to get shot at while local kids throw rocks and insults at you.

THE "JOB TRAINING" MYTH

The military likes to claim that you will be getting fun work in technology fields for the jobs of tomorrow. Recruiters promise you training that will lead to better jobs in civilian life. Which sounds great, right? You get paid while someone else trains you. **Except that veterans typically earn 12% to 15% less than those workers who do not go into the military.** Military training is designed for military jobs and most of the skills you do learn are particular to your military job. Only 12% of male veterans and 6% of female veterans report making any use of skills they learned in the military in subsequent civilian jobs. To make it even worse, even if you do get trained in the field you requested the military doesn't have to use you in that field. You might sign up to fly planes and end up being a mail clerk. Dick Cheney said it best, The military is not a social welfare agency; it's not a jobs program.

WOMEN IN THE MILITARY

A recent survey found **that 30% of women reported being victims of rape or attempted rape while in the military.** 75% reported being sexually harassed. Furthermore, survivors usually have little recourse when such crimes do occur. The machismo culture and closed environment of military life combined with threats and pressure from above makes it difficult to break the wall of silence.

DUDE, WHERE'S MY RIGHTS?

Counterrecruitment folding brochure spread — side 2
Created by the Pittsburgh Organizing Group

- If you leave your work without permission, you can be arrested
- Any disobedience can result in criminal punishment
- You can be punished without the right to see a lawyer or have a trial
- Your right to say what you think when and how you want will be restricted
- Individual expression through the way you dress and wear your hair is restricted
- You will be subject to routine urine tests for drugs

OTHER FACTS AND FIGURES

Military life is very hard on families; family abuse and violence are three to five times higher than in the civilian population.

The hazards of military service include more than just getting killed or wounded. Less than 300 U.S. soldiers were killed in the first Gulf War of 1991. But **tens of thousands** of Gulf War vets have reported **chronic, debilitating physical and psychological disorders** since serving in the Gulf.

Veterans comprise 1/3 of the adult homeless population in this country. If you're curious why, try asking a recruiter that question the next time they tell you enlisting is the right move for your future.

THERE'S NO PROMISE LIKE A GOVERNMENT PROMISE

The fine print on the back of the enlistment contract makes it clear that **no promise made by the government has to be kept.** The Military Enlistment/Reenlistment contract states: The following statements [in the contract] are not promises or guarantees of any kind.

Indeed, in 1995 the government stopped providing free healthcare for 20-year military retirees. This broke a promise made by recruiters (and in military brochures and advertisements) to generations of recruits. When veterans sued to force the government to fulfill its promise Bush's lawyers argued that it wasn't a legally binding promise because it had only been made by recruiters...

YOU'RE NOT OUT TILL THEY SAY YOU'RE OUT

Despite the stated length of enlistment, usually 4 years, recruits can be kept in the military indefinitely, or called back from the reserves many years later as we're seeing now with the current back door draft (a.k.a. "Stop loss.")

HOW TO GET RECRUITERS OFF YOUR BACK

Ever wonder where recruiters get so much personal information about you? Well, Federal Law means that your high school has to give them your personal information unless you say not to. Unfortunately many schools don't do an adequate job of letting you know you can opt-out of releasing the info thus avoiding some of those annoying calls and mailings to you and your parents. To print up an opt-out form, go to www.organizepittsburgh.org/opt_out.pdf and return the form to your principle or administer.

THERE ARE OTHER OPTIONS!

No one can tell you what the right post-graduate option is for you. Finding your calling in life is not an easy thing. Ideally you'll find something personally rewarding that is also compatible with your monetary and spiritual needs. Too often however we end up taking the easy way out and following a future someone else has picked out for us. This is YOUR future, follow your dreams. Just because there isn't a non-military recruiter at school providing you info on how to get where you want to go doesn't mean the info and opportunities aren't out there.

For a full list of resources on post-high school options, whether that means continuing your education, serving your community, job training, or starting a career now, see www.organizepittsburgh.org.

College: Don't assume you can't afford tuition, there's a lot of help out there. The less your family's income, the more grants and aid you'll likely receive.

Major grant/aid programs: www.finaid.org/fafsa
Scholorships: www.college-scholarships.com
www.collegeboard.com/pay

Other ways to serve your country:

Job Corps: a no-cost education and vocational training program that helps young people 16-24 get a better job, make more money and take control of their lives. http://jobcorps.doleta.gov/students.cfm

AmeriCorps: a network of national service programs that engage Americans in intensive service to meet critical needs in education, public safety, health, and the environment. www.americorps.org

From "Mixed Signals", a counterrecruitment tool in comic book form. Available to activists, teachers and others, from peacecomic@yahoo.com

TACTICS IN THE COMMUNITY

Visual Resistance

Recruiters saturate communities in many ways, including billboards, ads on Greyhound bus ticket envelopes, and displays in stores, community centers, and public spaces. Many community activists counter this by working to remove or alter these visuals, and, more importantly, by making their own campaigns visible.

Marie Skoczylas from the Pittsburgh Organizing Project describes how they counter these visibility campaigns: "One of my favorite tactics is to go into local businesses that have military displays or brochures and ask owners to take them down. I like it because it's something that everyone can do, it only takes a few minutes, and it's something that seems small but can have a big impact. Businesses are customer-service oriented and if they hear that possible patrons might be turned away, they'll usually oblige your request. I feel that it is important to create an unwelcoming environment for recruiters to operate, to spread the idea that militarism is not "normal" or desirable in our communities, and to limit the availability of the military's propaganda and the recruiters' accessibility to possible recruits."[99]

Here are some ways you can resist visually:

Stickers

Making and putting up stickers—words and/or images on adhesive paper or vinyl—is a fun and effective way to get a message out, and to challenge military ads, recruitment centers, and the like. Stickers create visibility for groups, movements, ideas, and images, and challenge or change the visual takeover of our surroundings by the military and corporate media.

How to:

Decide on your basic messages and images. Using a computer or marker, design simple, clear, and legible stickers. Make a sheet of designs on an 8½ by 11 inch piece of paper. You can fit four, six, or eight on a sheet. Once you have a design, make copies onto sticker paper available at many copy shops—possibly in color—and cut them into individual stickers.

You can buy cheap colored sticker paper from paper or office supply distributors. Industrial-strength sticker paper, nearly impossible to get off a clean dry surface, is also available if you search around office of paper supply stores or the internet. You can even get stickers professionally printed in large quantities—check local printers, or the internet.

Then, give them out to friends and supporters, or stick them up yourself in visible places. If possible, spraying fixative from an art store or clear spray enamel will seal the sticker so it won't run when wet. It is easy to saturate a campus in this way so that no one can get to class without seeing your message.

Billboard Alteration

From putting up your own images and messages to adbusting or altering those already up, billboard alteration has become very popular.

The Billboard Liberation Front explains the proliferation of billboards and advertising:

> Larger than life, subtle as war, they assault your senses with a complex coda of commercial instructions, the

> messenger RNA of capitalism. Every time you get in a car, ride a bus, or witness a sporting event, you receive their instructions. You can't run and you can't hide, because your getaway route is lined to the horizon with signs.

The Billboard Liberation Front how-to manual has a lot of good advice on how to go about "correcting" a billboard. You can view it at: www.billboardliberation.com/guidebook.html. However, they advise, "In most cases, it should not be necessary to follow the elaborate, even obsessive precautions we outline here. A can of spray paint, a blithe spirit, and a balmy night are all you really need.[100]

Postering

Public mass distributions of our message through postering—putting up posters with a written and/or visual message in public places—is one of the most direct, unmediated forms of expression available to us. Like the public postering of ideas and messages on the "democracy wall" during the 1989 Chinese prodemocracy movement, postering is a democratic public expression that can involve, stimulate, and engage people.

Los Angeles Guerrilla Posterer Robbie Canal explains postering as follows:

> Empowerment to take direct cooperative action on an issue that concerns us.
>
> For the general public who feel they have no avenues of resistance to the dominant power structure, no community support system, no ability to change their situation. To change apathy and cynicism to optimism.[101]

How to:

Make your poster image clear, provocative and readable from a distance. Remember, it's a poster, and you can't fit everything you think on it! Keep it simple. Make it on porous, light weight, nonglossy paper, like regular copy paper.

How to wheatpaste it:

- Wallpaper paste: Buy liquid wallpaper paste (easiest) or powder wallpaper paste (cheapest). Add one part Elmer's Glue to ten parts paste if you want to make it a bit more durable and water/rain-proof. Increase the amount of Elmer's Glue, or switch to waterproof wood glue, to make it more permanent—especially for nonporous surfaces like glass, Plexiglas, or painted flat surfaces.
- Cornstarch: Mix one tablespoon of powdered cornstarch with one cup of cold water. Mix until completely dissolved. Transfer to a small saucepan and heat over medium heat. Cook, stirring often, until the cornstarch starts to bubble and becomes transparent. Pour in a container and let cool. Be careful, it will be very hot!

Photo by Jeff Paterson, Jeff.Paterson.net

- Evaporated milk: A more low-key alternative for smaller posters is to use one part evaporated milk and one part water in a liquid spray bottle.

Apply the wheatpaste to the surface area, put the poster on, and using your hands, a brush, or a roller, smooth it so that it adheres to the surface. Apply another coat over it. It can help to practice at home on plywood, a box, or the like.

STENCILS

Stencils are cut outs of images and/or words on paper, cardstock, cardboard, and the like, that can be used to spray paint, or even brush paint, multiple images anywhere you like to communicate ideas, messages, questions, images, or critiques. They can be used on walls, sidewalks, t-shirts, or fabric patches, among other places.

Design:

Like with stickers and posters, make your stencil image simple, clear, and readable from a distance. You can design it on a computer, or by hand, or find an image and enlarge or reduce it at a copy shop. Copying it or printing it will allow you to cut it directly. For a larger stencil, you can design on more than one sheet by taping pieces together. You can even use a manila folder, cardstock, or cardboard (though it can be difficult to cut). For more durability, have it laminated first. Make sure there is enough paper area connecting letter and images so they are not too thin or fragile and will stay intact. If you will be spray-painting in a hurry, heavier, more durable paper or cardboard is best. Keep in mind that you cannot have any enclosed white spaces or "islands" inside any black areas, because essentially these black areas are what you will be cutting out.

Cut:

Use an exacto knife (best), utility/carpet knife, or box cutter with sharp blades (be careful!). In case you cut too far, have tape and glue handy for repairs. Also be sure to have adequate protection underneath your stencil to avoid damaging whatever you're cutting on.

Backing:

If you will be stenciling in public and want to be less visible, you can tape or glue your stencil to the bottom of a box or heavy shopping bag.

Painting:

Traditionally, with most street-based stencils, spray paint has been used as a quick and economical means to apply the image to street walls. If you are using spray paint for t-shirts or posters, make sure you have good ventilation. Try and use a quality flat (not glossy) paint, as it will last much longer and avoids any unwanted glare and reflections on your stencil that can occur from using glossy paints. Some folks wear latex gloves to keep their hands clean and avoid being caught red-handed—available at home-improvement and hardware stores.

Hold the can about a foot away and spray directly facing the stencil while moving the can to avoid too much paint or dripping. When applying your stencil to the wall, sidewalk, or wherever you are going to spray it, make sure it is as flat against the surface as possible to avoid underspray and to keep your lines crisp. You will find that, after a number of sprays, the stencil will harden as the paint layers dry and strengthen your stencil.

The best and most interesting work comes about when the image and its placement on the streets play together—the architecture and image communicating as one.

Stenciling on public or private property is a more serious risk than wheatpasting posters, so think about risks, be cautious, keep alert and calm.

WARNING: Altering private property or putting up art in public or private spaces may come with legal consequences.

TIPS FOR NOT GETTING ARRESTED OR HASSLED:

- Find out what the laws are and what people's actual experiences are in your area. Make a conscious decision about what risks you and your friends are willing to take. Keep in mind that having contact info or your group's name on your art, or just being very visible in your community around the issue, could incriminate you.
- Have an idea of where you are going—ideally even the exact spots you are targeting. Putting posters on businesses or homes may increase the risk, or may not feel appropriate. Have a phone number written on your arm or somewhere on your body (in case you are arrested and your stuff is taken) of someone you can call for support if you get in trouble—but not another posterer's cell phone.
- Carry posters and wheatpaste in a not-too-obvious way—hide everything in a shopping bag, backpack, or shoulder bag. Big posters can be carried in a tube.
- Keep your eyes open. Better yet, have a friend or several friends serve as look-out. If you are seen or stopped, move on, maybe to another neighborhood.
- Decide when you want to do it. There are fewer people around late at night, but you may also stand out or look suspicious.
- Be polite to everyone on the streets at night, including the police! Don't be hostile. A common response when stopped is, "It's an art project." Going to jail could ruin your evening.
- Be confident, stay calm, and enjoy.

Theater

Performance art uses your body to make your campaign visible in a creative way. There is no limit to what kinds of performances you may act out. What follows are some ideas that may help you get started.

Street Theater

Street theater—simple, direct, easy-to-understand theater performed in public spaces—is a great way to get a message out and have fun. In addition to the performers, folks can be involved by helping to draw a crowd, and handing out information at the end. Practice the lines, change them so they feel right, face the audience or wherever folks are at, and practice projecting so you can be heard over whatever is going on loud and clear. You can make or find costumes and/or you can do it with clearly visible nametags around the neck, or on hats. Challenge yourself. Have fun.

Popular-Education Theater

Forum Theater and How to Use it in Counterrecruiting

By Levana Saxon

Forum Theater was created by Augusto Boal from Brazil to inspire dialogue and action among communities facing a common oppressor. It's a powerful tool that anyone can use to rehearse and talk about possible solutions to complicated problems. In its most basic form it's a loosely structured skit with a bad ending that is performed twice. The second time the audience can at any point yell "Freeze!" and jump on stage, replace or add a character, and attempt to change things for the better.

One of the more obvious lessons of Forum Theater is that the oppressions we face will just keep playing themselves out until people are willing to jump up and change things.

Fundamental to this work is the dual meaning of the word 'act': to perform and take action. As the audience or "spectactors" begin to act themselves, they are in effect taking action to critically analyze and rehearse problems in their lives so that action offstage seems more possible.

Usually the main character is subject to various oppressions throughout the skit that the audience can identify with, and usually the audience can only replace the characters who they feel are the most oppressed. I say usually because as Forum Theater adapts to fit complex power dynamics in different contexts around the world, the traditional rules blur.

Along with Forum Theater, Augusto Boal developed an entire arsenal of theater practices called "Theater of the Oppressed." He contrasts his theater with Aristotle's theater, or bourgeois theater, which he says functions to reproduce elite vision of the world and to pacify "the people," or spectators. He calls bourgeois theater finished

Int'l Capoeira Angola Foundation perform outside the Oakland, CA Recruiting Center. 2006. Photo by Jeff Paterson, Jeff.Paterson.net

theater; the bourgeoisie already knows what the world is like, and they simply present it on stage. In contrast to this, the working classes or the "masses" do not yet know what their world will be like, therefore their theater is unfinished. As such, it can provide space for people to rehearse different possible outcomes.

Forum Theater is an obvious tool in counterrecruitment work. A lot of youth are under all kinds of pressures to enlist from family, from school counselors, from recruiters, from friends, from pop culture, and so on. Having a supportive space to rehearse saying no to all these different pressures can make saying no in real life easier.

Last year I was working with a multiracial group of educators and artists called Student Theater Educators for Peaceful Solutions (STEPS). We created a ten-minute Forum Theater piece about military recruitment that we performed at a counterrecruitment conference and at a public high school in Oakland. In the skit this kid we'll call Jerry is about to graduate high school and is approached by a military recruiter who tries to be his new best friend and tells him all kinds of lies. Then his real best friend comes by to tell him that she just signed up and can't wait to make all the money that will come with it and that he should sign up too, so that he can finally buy a decent pair of shoes. Then he goes to see his school counselor about college. She won't give him the time of day, much less scholarship information, but tells him to sign up for the military because his grades aren't good enough for scholarships. Then he goes home and his dad lays into him about needing to bring home more money and suggests he join the military. At the end, Jerry decides to join up and is killed in combat.

When we presented this to different classes at a public high school in Oakland, people were jumping out of their seats. Many of the students said that they could definitely relate. As low-income youth of color, the only future they were encouraged to imagine was jail or the military.

During the second performance students yelled "freeze" at almost every instant of the play. When the recruiter was showing off his new Hummer, saying that Jerry could have one too if he just signed up, someone jumped up and stole the Hummer to demonstrate that material possessions are temporary and not worth risking your life for. Other people tried adding a counterrecruiter to the scene who had a military fact sheet with him. When his best friend came up and started pressuring him to sign up, different people tried replacing the Jerry character to talk him out of it and expose to him the lies that he was told. When he went to see the school counselor, students replaced Jerry and talked back to him, snatched scholarship information, and demanded community college information. They also added an administrator to watch the counselor do her job right, and added another teacher to help with the workload so that she would have more time. When Jerry went home and spoke with his father, people again replaced him and gave a couple of incredibly moving performances as sons standing up to their fathers and standing up for their own dreams.

I think Forum is really natural and easy, and can be done by anyone almost anywhere, but because of all the fancy language around it, a lot of people are intimidated. Even my second-grade students created their own Forum Theater without my prompting. We were improvising a restaurant scene in which one of the waitresses was letting the other waitress lie about her and get her fired. When she didn't stand up for herself, almost everyone else in the class was jumping up and down with their hands up, begging to let them stop the skit and take her place. Everyone had a turn, and it was brilliant.

I don't mean to suggest that Forum Theater is simple. There are incredible complexities to doing this work. I've been working with it for ten years and I'm still learning new aspects all of the time. However, it can be simplified to its basic parts so that anyone with little to no theater or teaching experience can use it. Here's one suggested format:

- Step one:
  Pick a main character who:
  - is spineless, pathetic, and being oppressed by everyone else in the skit;
  - is dealing with problems that the audience can identify with.
- Step two:
  Identify other characters who:
  - have really obvious ways in which they are being oppressive;
  - sometimes do not know they are being oppressive;
  - sometimes are also being oppressed;
  - use physical motions a lot—they "do" things on stage, not just talk.
- Step three:
  Create a storyboard:
  - Draw a big grid with six to nine spaces and write in the basic idea of each scene in each box; i.e. box one: recruiter pounces on kid outside of Best Buy, talks about car, college, benefits.
- Step four:
  Cast characters and improvise the whole thing, with the storyboard visible for all to reference. This is important to do before too much talking takes place. It's much easier to create a Forum Theater piece by acting it out than it is by talking it out.

- Step five:
  A Joker is selected who prepares to facilitate the performance, and becomes familiar with the "rules of the game."
- Step six:
  Rehearse, rehearse, rehearse!
- Step seven:
  Perform, and then Joker it:
  - At the beginning of the performance, people should be told that they will see it twice and that they may intervene the second time.
  - Perform it.
  - Joker comes out and invites the audience to take a minute to talk to the person next to them about what they saw and what they wanted to see. Joker could also do some warm-up activities with the audience.
  - Joker then explains the rules of the game.
  - It is performed again, but this time when someone yells "freeze!" they come up on stage. The Joker then asks the person where they want to start the scene from. The other actors stay in character and intensify their oppression, but if the intervention successfully affects them, they should allow themselves to be affected and show it. After the intervention is complete, the scene continues from right before the last intervention until another "freeze!" is yelled, and so on.

Rules of the Game

- Do not tell us what the main character should do, show us!
- You may replace anyone who you identify with (how you identify with that person or her problem is up to the discretion of the spectator).

- You may add a character.
- No magic is allowed (for example, unless there is a military recruiter in the audience, no one can replace the military recruiter and suddenly decide to be honest).
- There are no right or wrong interventions even magical ones are useful because they inspire good dialogue about what is and what is not possible.

Notes on Jokering:

The Joker is not a facilitator but a difficultator—she works to make things difficult. She does not offer suggestions but instead only poses questions to the audience: "Was that magic?" "Can we do this is real life?" She also poses questions to the intervening spect-actor: "Are you done with your intervention?" "What was your intervention?" "How is it working for you?" Depending on time constraints, the Joker should ask a lot of questions, as one of the main objectives of Forum Theater is to inspire dialogue.

To learn more, read *Games for Actors and Non-Actors* by Augusto Boal.

Levana Saxon is an educator and antiwar organizer who uses theater, puppets, and ecopedagogy, a radical approach to education for the earth. She has worked with Youth for Environmental Sanity, the Paulo Freire Institute (IPF), PEACE (Popular Education and Action Collective), cofounded the Indigenous and Non-Indigenous Youth Alliance, and now is the youth educator for Rainforest Action Network.

San Francisco's College Not Combat Voter Initiative

Fine. You want to be your own country? Go right ahead. And if al Qaeda comes in here and blows you up, we're not going to do anything about it. We're going to say, look, every other place in America is off limits to you except San Francisco. You want to blow up the Coit Tower? Go ahead.
—Bill O'Reilly[102]

Growing opposition to the war and to recruitment on public school campuses has led to efforts at the ballot box. In December 2004 an upsurge of counterrecruitment actions took place on college campuses across the nation, from Seattle Community College to San Francisco State. Universally, college administrations took a hard line. Students and organizations were threatened with expulsion and were roughed up by campus police. In San Francisco the College Not Combat campaign was born to prove that students had broad support for challenging military recruitment on campuses.

To start, they gathered a diverse group of one-hundred people, including lawyers from the National Lawyers Guild, antiwar groups, campus groups, parent groups, and community organizations. Campaign leader Todd Creitian explains, "We'd done our homework—San Francisco has a relatively accessible way to get a proposition on the ballot. We put out the general idea of a ballot measure but it took two months to figure out the technicalities. The original idea was to raise a progressive tax in the city to fund scholarships for poor students as a way to pay for their education instead of joining the military. Legal barriers including the statewide Proposition 13 prevented us from including this provision.

COURAGE
TO
RESIST!

At age 19 I enlisted in the Guard as a cook because I wanted to experience military life. When I enlisted I believed that killing was immoral, but also that war was an inevitable part of life and therefore, an exception to the rule.

After enlisting I began the slow transformation into adulthood.

I began to see a bigger picture of the world and I started to reevaluate everything that I had been taught about war as a child. I developed the belief that taking human life was wrong and war was no exception.

Because I believe so strongly in non violence, I cannot perform any role in the military. Any person doing any job in the Army contributes in some way to the planning, preparation or implementation of war.

Army SPC Katherine Jashinski
the first woman to publicly declare resistance to participation in the Iraq War

ARMY OF NONE

So we settled on language for a resolution against privileged recruiter access to public schools in the city."

The group had just seven weeks to gather 15,000 signatures. They began with a kick-off event with 150 people who took petitions out for eight hours. That was followed by a series of weekend mobilizations that gathered an average of 2,500 signatures a week. Todd recalls, "We found these to be easy signatures to get—about eight out of ten people asked signed the petition. Because supermarkets and malls prohibit gathering signatures under the Patriot Act, we had to find public locations with lots of people and that was a challenge. In all, it was a tremendous effort.

"At the same time, we did a simultaneous press campaign that brought veterans and war resisters to endorse the proposition. We held musical events as fundraisers to pay for the signs, buttons, and fliers. We brought together activists to visit every public high school on the last day of the school year. The proposition quickly became a national issue, bringing military recruiting to the forefront of debate. We demonstrated concretely that the population in the city is fed up with war and targeting our young people for recruitment in the schools."

But Todd cautions counterrecruitment groups to carefully weigh the pros and cons of this approach. "Like any tactic, this approach can be useful or not useful. You must do your homework and be clear about what you're trying to accomplish. If possible, don't prioritize electoral campaigns for counterrecruitment, but consider it part of an overall strategy. The tactic can be useful depending on the strength of your coalition."[103]

In all, the success of the College Not Combat ballot initiative was more than just a symbolic protest against military recruiting. In Todd's estimation, the campaign helped to train a new generation of antiwar activists.

In addition, citywide efforts speak to a great audience, and can ultimately help to change dialogues around war and recruitment on a national level.

SOME TIPS BEFORE YOU PROCEED:

- Conduct a legal analysis of ballot access laws—some cities are easier than others. In Seattle, you need three times as many signatures to get a ballot measure than in San Francisco.
- Consider fundraising to fund buttons and signs.
- Explore whether a friendly local elected official will present an antirecruitment resolution as an alternative to a ballot initative.
- Create a media strategy to explain the value of cities taking a position against recruitment. Publish op-eds, write letters to the editor, and present alternative and mainstream media outlets with students' and parents' stories. These are very compelling to reporters.

Direct Action Against Military Recruitment and War

What is Direct Action?

Direct action means using our bodies, voices, and creativity to directly confront injustice. Shutting down a recruitment center or sitting-in at a power holder's office is a form of direct action, as is refusing to deploy to Iraq.

Direct action allows those taking part to establish ownership over the process of change. Creating a space for people to directly confront injustice can empower people and build community and momentum like no other means. Direct participation to attain tangible goals inspires political involvement and long-term dedication, plain and simple.

Nonviolent direct action has been an essential part of every successful social change movement in United States history. The slavery abolition movement, women's suffrage, campaigns for workers' rights, the black civil-rights movement, and antiwar, environmental justice, human rights, AIDS justice, and housing and human-needs campaigns all owe much of their success to this kind of activism. In fact, direct action has played a key role in overthrowing unpopular dictators and presidents in recent decades—from the Philippines, to Indonesia, to the former Soviet bloc governments, and to Bolivia, Ecuador, and Argentina.

Activists blockade and wheatpaste paper banners over the windows of the Oakland, CA Recruiting Center as Peace and Justice Movement Recruitment tables are set up outside. After continuing protest, the Recruitment Center moved out of the city. International Consciencious Objectors Day, May 15, 2006. Photo by Jeff Paterson, Jeff.Paterson.net

When the established channels for change fail—which they so often do—people everywhere assert their democratic right to be involved in the decisions that impact their lives by engaging in direct action. Sit-ins, blockades, occupations, strikes, walkouts, and other nonviolent methods are all examples of direct action. When part of a campaign—a series of related activities to achieve certain goals—direct action can be a powerful, and often essential, ingredient in winning change. See Stages of a Direct Action Campaign (page 161) to think about how it might fit into a more powerful campaign strategy.

Putting our bodies on the line and directly confronting and intervening in recruitment and war is a key part of the counterrecruitment and antiwar movements. Here are some stories of antiwar and counter military recruitment campaigns which have effectively and creatively employed nonviolent direct action as part of their campaigns.

Confronting a Recruiting Center and Standing Up to Repression: Pittsburgh Organizing Group

The youth-led community-based Pittsburgh Organizing Project (POG) of Pittsburgh, Pennsylvania, despite meeting an incredibly repressive response, has had much success result from demonstrations and direct actions at the Oakland neighborhood recruiting station.

Marie Skoczylas of the Pittsburgh Organizing Project describes the campaign:

> POG's campaign to counter military recruitment has been going on for over a year. It has included more than thirty pickets at our local recruiting hub station, direct actions that have shut the station down, presentations and skill shares in other cities,

educational outreach at local high schools, a petition to restrict access of military recruiters at area schools, a conference that brought counterrecruitment activists from other cities across the country together to share skills and strategies, and actions that confronted recruiters on campuses and in the streets.

We chose to focus on counterrecruitment specifically after a few years of doing more general antiwar work (such as planning rallies and marches against the war and U.S. imperialism) because we wanted to work on something more concrete and we realized we could have the most impact doing it from a personal standpoint. Many of us have been targeted by recruiters; some of us have friends and family who ended up joining the military. We realized we could have an impact on how successful the military can be signing up people in our own city, sending them oversees to kill and be killed. We felt that opposing recruitment is one of the only tangible

Activists line the sidewalk outside a recruiting station near the University of Pittsburgh as part of a counterrecruitment conference organized by Pittsburgh Organizing Group. Photo by David Meieran, organizepittsburgh.org

ways that it's realistic for the antiwar movement to end this and future wars. We can be out there in the streets in Washington, D.C., or New York with millions of people saying we're against the war. But targeting recruitment here in Pittsburgh is a way we can have an impact at home. We like to say that we're really trying to make it an "army of one."

Our campaign utilizes both education and direct action. I feel as though the direct action element has been important in setting an example in our city for other groups, breaking down the stereotype that it has to be just one or the other. Some local groups are much more comfortable with necessary confrontation now than they had been before. Many of us in POG feel a responsibility to not only voice dissent but to actively work to change unjust situations. The government and certain corporations benefit from war. No amount of asking nicely will get them to change their actions. We have to use our voices

Photo by David Meieran, organizepittsburgh.org

and actively take steps to go for what we want. The recruiters are using deceptive tactics to get people to enlist? We shut the station down so they can't do their work. Recruiters are preying on students on campus? We block them from the public view with a banner and hand out information dispelling their myths and offering alternatives to military service.

The Pentagon Department of Defense database has labeled POG as a threat to national security—citing our very first counterrecruitment action. Undercover agents film us from an abandon storefront window at our pickets in front of the recruiting station. At our last march, riot cops lined the sidewalks along with fences separating protesters from the public. There was a helicopter, K-9 units, horse brigades, motorcycle cops, bike cops, numerous undercovers, snatch squads, and special surveillance vans roaming the streets. At one of our demonstrations last August, police pepper-sprayed protesters (hitting some young children and their parents), allowed a police dog to bite a sixty-eight-year-old woman, and tasered two individuals in attendance that day.

When the police and government crack down, we use it to draw public attention to our issue. For example, when the police get violent at a demonstration, suddenly reporters and talk show hosts want to hear what we have to say. We use it to get the message out about countering recruitment. The more the government cracks down on our organizing, the more we know we're doing something right. We just try to use it to our advantage.

I really enjoy our regular pickets. They not only provide another place to do outreach about the realities of military service and show persistent resistance to recruiters' practices, but they provide a space for new people to get involved. The regular pickets

> enable new folks to feel empowered by immediately taking some sort of action and they provide a space for those of us who have been doing counterrecruitment work to get to know new people. It's much more effective at building the movement than inviting new people to a three-hour planning meeting.

Kicking Recruiters Off Campus: UC Santa Cruz

On three occasions Students Against War (SAW) at the University of California has prevented the military from recruiting at UCSC career fairs, meaning that the military hasn't been able to recruit there for almost two years. This is because each time, protesters have surrounded the recruiters, blocking their efforts, and twice have removed them from the premises.

SAW activist Sam Aranke speaks of their campaign:

> Counterrecruitment has been a foundational part of UCSC Students Against War since the group came together in January 2005. We look for projects which allow us to resist war, while demilitarizing our community. Our counterrecruitment campaign has focused primarily on banning military recruiters from our campus. Through direct action and education, we make it impossible for the campus community to ignore the role our university plays in war.[104]

David Zlutnick, a student and fellow member of SAW, explains the importance of nonviolent direct action:

> SAW was founded on this principle, that we must be the change we want to see. If the student government wants to pass a resolution against military recruiters we will gladly accept their support, but that won't make recruiters stop coming. If we want them off our campus we must force them off.[105]

The success of SAW has hinged primarily on its belief in direct action, its refusal to be co-opted into the school's bureaucracy, and its refusal to compromise on its beliefs. If we want to see a world without war, without militaries, based on our collective voice and direct participation, then we must build it ourselves.

Sam explains how they have dealt with the authorities:

> Police and university administration have consistently worked together in an attempt to squash SAW's antiwar efforts. At first, members of our group agreed to meet with the administration as temporary representatives. We entered the meeting with projects and long-term strategy proposals around the Solomon Amendment, which at this time was still up for debate. Upon entering the meeting, we realized that the administration had completely different goals in mind. They attempted to pinpoint us as leaders of the group, even though we are committed to nonhierarchical organizing and do not have leaders. For the administration, cooperation meant that members of our group assist them in policing our [group] and tell them of our future action plans.
>
> One major critique of that action was that it prevented students from getting jobs because the Administration shut down the career fair for about an hour and a half. In our future actions we paid more attention to the real need many students have to get jobs.
>
> The next fall, the University was ready for a repeat performance. They planned the fair at an inconvenient place and time so it would be impossible to mobilize the way we had in the spring. But we were undeterred. We had a more symbolic action planned to draw attention to the military's "don't ask, don't tell" rule, which violates the university's "nondiscrimination policy."

We surrounded the recruiters with a "queer-kiss-in." A dozen nonheterosexual kissing couples formed a wall in front of recruiters, effectively preventing recruiters from accessing students.

This spring, in preparation for the recruiters, SAW delivered a letter to the administration, with six demands to protect student protestors:

1. Police presence will be minimal and will not stand in the way of nonviolent protest.
2. Students will not face disciplinary actions for nonviolent protest.
3. Student IDs will not be collected.
4. Media will be allowed into the fair.
5. The military recruiters will be separated from other employers.
6. The date, time, and location of the fair, once announced, will not be changed.

If the University would agree to these suggestions, we promised, the career fair would be able to continue while we confronted the military recruiters. Even though the University refused to agree to these suggestions, on the day of the career fair (April 11, 2006), the recruiters were in a separate room. It was 9 a.m. and raining as sixty of us determinedly marched to the fair to confront the recruiters. We sat down outside of the doors to the room where the recruiters were. Through group negotiations with the administrators, eventually the recruiters left as we cheered.

Since news broke out that SAW was listed as a "credible threat" on the Pentagon's surveillance list of antiwar groups, we were certain that police—with the help of campus administration—provided information and resources on SAW and our actions.

All of this information led to our eventual partnership with the ACLU to retrieve all the information from the government about these Pentagon TALON reports.

As for the presence of police at counterrecruitment actions, we have used police liaisons. Police liaisons are designated members of SAW who volunteer to seek out police, keep in constant communication with them, but do not negotiate on behalf of the students. Liaisons keep the crowd aware of the attitudes, decisions, and general mood of the police—making sure that if the police start to talk about arrest, the crowd is fully aware of it.

Counterrecruitment actions like these are energizing and empowering in the larger struggle against war and militarism, when most of the things we do are far less sexy. It is important to be reminded that students can have power over administrators and the government. Given the many struggles we have yet to face, we continue to take the fight directly to the beast—regardless of campus administration or law enforcement.[106]

Raging Grannies Take Direct Action: Granny Enlistment Actions

Grandmas, let's unite
While we are still upright
Let's protest that parasite
Watch out! We've just begun to fight!
—Joan Wile, founder of Grandmothers Against the War

A proliferation of grandmother groups—Raging Grannies, Grandmothers for Peace, Grandmothers Against the War, and the Grannie Peace Brigade—have taken off in recent

Harlem Grandmothers Against the War protest on Tax Day, April 17, 2006 at the 125th St. Army Recruiting Office. Photo by Naomi Dagen Bloom, alittleredhen.com

years, challenging and embarrassing recruiters, and capturing the nation's imagination.

On July 13, 2005, eight grandmothers in colorful flowered hats marched into a Tucson, Arizona, recruitment station and attempted to enlist. Their action would help catalyze what the *Village Voice* called the "Granny Power" antiwar movement. The grandmothers sang a few songs (like "God Help America") and read a statement that said in part:

> The Raging Grannies want to enlist in the U.S. military forces to make possible the immediate return of all U.S. service personnel, and to set an example of what REAL diplomacy can achieve. We would meet with our counterparts in Iraq (women) and come to a mutual agreement of how best for Iraq

> to regain its own independence, as all U.S. troops, bases, and corporations leave their country.
>
> The Raging Grannies are angry about the U.S. military recruitment system that lies to young people about the reasons for needing more people in the military. We are angry that our young peoples' lives are at risk for reasons that have nothing to do with defending our country. We insist that recruiters tell the truth to our grandchildren who come to serve their country.

The recruiters threatened to press charges against what one described on the phone as "a room full of elderly ladies." The police arrived, arrested, and cited the grandmothers.

The grannies and others had been showing up in front of the military recruiting offices on Speedway Street each Wednesday morning since the war had begun and felt that it was time to step it up. Their action inspired many.

Second Action: October 17, 2005

"Grandmother struck me as a powerful word," Grandmothers Against the War founder Joan Wile told the *Village Voice*. "I thought that to see grandmothers on the street would impress people with the gravity of the situation." Wiles formed the New York City-based group, which holds weekly vigils in Rockefeller Center. Ms. Wile, a former cabaret singer and songwriter who wrote the original music to Lynn Redgrave's 1975 film *The Happy Hooker,* which explains her ease in writing and singing the trademark satirical songs the grannies are known for.

When she and others heard about the Tucson grannies' attempt to enlist, they decided to follow the example. "It's obviously the thing to do," seventy-eight-year-old Corrine Willinger told the *Voice*. [107]

On October 17 eighteen grandmothers attempted to enlist at the Times Square recruiting station. Backed by dozens of supporters, the grandmothers attempted to enter the recruiting station to enlist. Undeterred when recruiters locked the doors against them, they sat down in front, blocking the entrance, and were arrested.

The grandmothers were finally acquitted on April 27, 2006, after six months of legal proceedings and a trial that captured international media attention that made the prosecutors stuck with the job of trying to convict eighteen grandmothers look ridiculous. "Our goal was to put the war on trial, and I think we did that. Mission accomplished," said Wiles. Two months later the same New York Granny Peace Brigade led a Grannie Peace Brigade antiwar caravan to Washington, D.C. En route they took over the Philadelphia Recruiting Center on June 28, attempting again to enlist and talking to potential recruits who decided to think more before enlisting.

Valentines Day

Inspired by the October 17 arrest and jailing of the eighteen grandmothers in Times Square, New York City, the newly created Bay Area Grandmothers Against the War in Oakland, California, decided to follow their example on Valentine's Day—and their idea spread.

On Valentine's Day 2006 (termed "Valentine's Day De-Massacre" by one of the would-be recruits), grandmothers in at least fifteen cities across the United States engaged in enlistment actions at recruiting centers in an effort to replace young Americans being needlessly thrown away in Bush's horrendous illegal occupation of Iraq.

Many attempted to enlist, a few were arrested, some performed street theater, and all sang peace songs. The cities were representative of the entire country—Fresno and

Oakland, California, on the West Coast; Tucson, Arizona, in the Southwest; Detroit, Cleveland, and Minneapolis in the Midwest; Southern Florida, St. Augustine, and Sarasota Florida in the Southeast; Silver Spring, Maryland, in the South/Mid-Atlantic region; New York City, Albany, and Rochester, New York, and Pittsburgh, Pennsylvania, in the Northeast; and Barre, Vermont, in New England.

Vet Drops Banner: Ohio for Peace

Displays are a popular way for recruiters to get attention and intitiate contact with potential recruits. Here is the story of one activist who subverted such tactics. On October 29, 2005, Dave Airhart, a twenty-four-year-old Iraq and Afghanistan war veteran, scaled the climbing wall set up by military recruiters on the campus of Kent State University. When he reached the top, he unfurled a banner reading, "Kent, Ohio, for Peace." Twenty other students with the Kent State Antiwar Committee assembled to show their opposition to war and to military recruitment on their campus. Enraged by the banner, a military recruiter screamed, "Get the fuck off the tower!" and scrambled up the wall after Airhart, forcing the combat vet to ditch his harness and climb down the steel beams on the backside of the wall. Once on solid ground, the anthropology undergraduate was charged with disorderly conduct and threatened with expulsion.

Taking place on the same campus where National Guardsmen massacred four students at a Vietnam War protest in 1970, Airhart's action gathered national attention to the war and recruitment.

Airhart explained his action to *Rolling Stone*, "I wish that I could have had someone who had been in the military tell me, 'Hey, your recruiter is full of shit. He gets bonuses for recruiting people, so he'll do whatever it takes to get people to join.' It's like the rock-climbing wall they put up at Kent—what's that have to do with going to war?"[108]

Airhart's fellow activists quickly organized widespread public support, including an international petition campaign called Hands Off Dave. The pressure worked: the following month Kent State did an abrupt about-face, canceling Airhart's disciplinary hearing and dropping all charges against him.

Graphic credit: © 2006 Mica Semrick, www.artpolitic.org

Photo by Jeff Paterson, Jeff.Paterson.net

SECTION THREE

PEOPLE POWER AND STRATEGIC ORGANIZING

FOR A SUSTAINABLE MOVEMENT

Photo by Jeff Paterson, Jeff.Paterson.net

PEOPLE POWER STRATEGY TO END WAR AND BUILD A BETTER WORLD

It dawned on me after the election that people are tired of unfocused protests and calls to action with no strategy or concrete goals to work for.

—Mike Kress, an Air Force veteran and conscientious objector who now works with the Spokane Peace and Justice Action League

The world seems to be waiting for those of us in the United States—and millions of us here are ready—to finally stand up to the Bush administration and the bipartisan policies of empire. How will we actually stop the war and occupation?

In 2003 we tried to stop the invasion of Iraq, and in 2004 we tried to oust the invader. Both times, incredible groundswells of grassroots activism from nearly every sector of society hit the streets and doorsteps of the United States. We won important, though less visible, victories but failed on both counts. One reason it's been so hard to mobilize people after the invasion is that there is no clear logic as to where our efforts are headed. What will another march or even nonviolent direct action add up to? How will we actually stop the war and occupation? We have exhausted the established channels of change. Political pressure, lobbying, and elections have not worked. It's time for a different approach.

The antiwar movement needs a new strategy to stop the war and occupation of Iraq.

The solution is written in the mountain-road blockades and mass mobilizations in Bolivia that have driven out transnational corporations like Bechtel and Suez and even the country's president in 2003. It is written in the farm-worker-led Taco Bell boycott victory of 2005, and the immigration-rights boycotts, walkouts, and mobilizations. It's in our rewritten history. It's called people power.

People power is an assertion of real democracy. It asserts the democratic will of communities and movements to change the things that matter when the established so-called democratic channels turn out be little more than public relations for elite rule. Every successful movement in the United States, from the workers' and civil rights movements to victories in anticorporate campaigns today, and every dictator toppled in recent history, have relied on people power methods. The term was popularized by the 1986 Philippine uprising against the U.S.-backed dictator Ferdinand Marcos, in which military resistance and mass mobilizations were central to ousting him.

A people power analysis understands that power is not something that those in power hold but is a fragile relationship between those in power and the rest of us. Our compliance forms the pillars on which their power depends. When we withhold our cooperation and organize determined movements to intervene, we can assert our power and force changes—or remove those who refuse to make them.

If we adopt a people power strategic framework, identify the pillars that support the war, and choose thoughtful campaigns with creative tactics to remove them, then we will have a viable movement. People who do counterrecruitment organizing witness concrete victories everyday on a one-on-one level, and can see its potential to end the war and even stop the next one by cutting off the supply of soldiers. It is one key part of a bigger strategy. Doing this important work, while sharing the same overarching goal with other types of equally important justice work, will allow for all our efforts to cumulate into something very powerful. In this way, we may retain a sustaining sense of purpose as we achieve specific victories and milestones. In all of our steps we may engage in a long-term struggle for a fundamental revision of the United States foreign and domestic policies, for real democracy and against empire. Do we have the guts and imagination?

We are throwing a lot of words around here, so let's define the terms:

- **Strategic Framework:** a basic concept or plan for achieving longer-term goals.
- **Campaign:** a series of activities to achieve specific goals; these can be both short-range and long-range.
- **Tactics:** a specific action intending to get a particular result, often as part of a campaign.

In the lead-up to the 2003 United States invasion of Iraq, as the world protested and pressured the U.S. government to stop, some parts of the antiwar movements began to turn toward a people power approach. In Ireland a campaign of protest and direct action at Shannon Air Force Base successfully stopped it from being used as a major refueling stop for U.S. troop and supply flights on their way to Iraq. In Britain, dockworkers refused to load supplies for the U.S. war. In Italy, activists blocked trains moving supplies for the war. In Turkey, mass protest forced the government to refuse to let the nation be used as a staging base for the invasion, which U.S. war planners had taken for granted.

In San Francisco, the Bay Area Direct Action to Stop the War called for a next-day shutdown of the city's financial district if the United States invaded Iraq. The well-publicized goals of the shutdown said in part, "We will impose real economic, social, and political costs and stop business as usual until the war stops with the express intention of deterring a war in Iraq and future wars." A diverse San Francisco Bay Area antiwar movement united around this common framework. On March 19, 2003, the United States began its invasion. The next day the *San Francisco Chronicle* quoted San Francisco police officer Drew Cohen as saying, "They succeeded this morning—they shut the city down. They're highly organized but they are totally spontaneous. The protesters are always one step ahead of us." It worked because everyone understood and was operating within a common-strategy framework that made sense and had logic to it.

A Common-Strategy Framework

A common strategy framework is a shared sense of purpose that allows everyone to work together while doing what they can individually, complementary of one another's efforts.

It's clear that we are not all going to agree on any one (or two or three) campaigns, but it is possible for us to consciously adopt and promote a people power strategy that makes our various efforts complementary and cumulative. I think of it as a massive umbrella under which we can—whether we are a national organization, a local group, or a decentralized network—make our efforts add up.

"I left the military because the situation is now that it is not conducting itself as a professional unit. I refuse to work in an organization that commits war crimes."

"At the end of the day, you have to ask yourself if this is something you can live with. It's your life and the choice is ultimately yours to make. I said NO and I will never regret it."

— KYLE SNYDER

"It is my conclusion as an officer of the Armed Forces that the war in Iraq is not only morally wrong but a horrible breach of American law. Although I have tried to resign out of protest, I am forced to participate in a war that is manifestly illegal. As the order to take part in an illegal act is ultimately unlawful as well, I must as an officer of honor and integrity refuse that order."

— LIEUTENANT EHREN WATADA

Lt. Ehren Watada (with Iraq Veterans Against the War behind him) addresses the National Veterance for Peace Conference, 2006. Photo by Jeff.Paterson, Jeff.Paterson.net

Here are a few key elements that made the short-term people power actions in San Francisco at the start of the Iraq War successful:

- Clear What-and-Why Logic: Shut down the Financial District in order to impose a cost on war.
- Broadly Publicized: Repeated lead-up actions and press conferences, street art, tens of thousands of fliers, a widely utilized web site and broad community mobilizing made sure a huge portion of the Bay Area knew what was planned and why.
- Mass Training and Mass Organization: A few thousand people received civil-disobedience trainings at schools, churches, and rallies, and well over a thousand people were directly involved in the organizing via affinity groups, working groups, and public meetings.
- Decentralization: Many allied groups who had minimal contact with the initiating organization understood and supported the strategy, and participated in the action without coming to an organizing meeting or bothering to identify as part of the organizing nucleus, "Direct Action to Stop the War."

What if we, locally, nationally, or internationally, had agreed on a long-term people power strategy before the war started in Iraq? What if we were not just trying to have our voices heard in order to influence those in power, but were actually asserting our own power and withdrawing the pillars of support for war and empire-building policies? What if we do it now?

Pillars of War

A group of people in a college campus classroom are participating in a "people power strategy to end the war" workshop. They are asked to "think of what are the pillars of support that the U.S. war in Iraq depend on—which, if you removed them, the war and occupation could not continue?" "Troops," someone shouts out. That person is asked to step forward and become that pillar by holding up part of a mattress with the words war and occupation of Iraq taped to it. Another person says, "Corporations, like Halliburton." That person becomes the second pillar holding up the war and occupation mattress. "Media—that persuades people to support the war and misinforms them." The person steps forward, and the mattress has three pillars.

The workshop facilitator asks, "What are some ways we can weaken or remove these pillars of support—let's start

Photo by Jeff Paterson, Jeff.Paterson.net

with troops?" "Counterrecruiting, so they can't get enough soldiers." "Supporting soldiers who refuse," someone else offers. "Resisting a military draft that they might turn to if we are successful at counterrecruiting."

"If we do all these things, will that weaken or remove the pillar of troops?" People agree that it could, and so that pillar is removed and the mattress lurches, held up by just two pillars. The same exercise is done with the "corporate" and "media" pillars. The mattress collapses.

What are the key pillars of support—the sources of power without which the war and occupation could not continue? Three key pillars are soldiers, corporations, and media disinformation. While they are not the exclusive list of pillars people might identify, here's an explanation of why they are key and what effective campaign/s might look like:

Pillar of War: Troops

The United States government can't fight war or maintain an occupation without enough troops—or without obedient troops. Nor can it begin new wars. This pillar could be weakened if we:

Counterrecruit to reduce the military's ability to recruit young people

As you have been learning about in this book, students and community members across the United States have taken spirited action and waged legal and political challenges that have driven military recruiters from their campuses and communities. Massive countereducation of students and youth, mounting protest and direct action at recruiting centers, and increasing resistance in the Army reserves have contributed (along with the losing war in Iraq) to low military recruitment.

Develop campaigns that support troops and National Guard (or private or government employees) who refuse deployment or orders, in compliance with international law

GI resistance within the military, together with mass desertion and draft resistance, is widely credited with being a key element in forcing the United States out of Vietnam. David Zeiger, director of the recent Vietnam GI resistance movement film, *Sir, No Sir!*, and active organizer in the antiwar GI coffeehouse-related solidarity efforts, describes the movement:

> Like the Vietnam War itself, the GI Antiwar Movement started small and within a few years had exploded into a force that altered history. And like the times from which it grew, the movement involved organized actions and spontaneous resistance, political groups and cultural upheaval. Between 1966 and 1975, groups of soldiers—some small and some numbering in the thousands—emerged to challenge the war and racism in the military. Group action and individual defiance, from the 500,000 GIs who deserted over the course of the war to the untold numbers who wore peace signs, defied military discipline and avoided combat, created a "Fuck the Army" counter culture that threatened the entire military culture of the time and changed the course of the war.[109]

Lt. Ehren Watada, the first commissioned officer to publicly refuse deployment to Iraq, asserted the power of GI Resistance to stop the war and occupation in Iraq and the importance of civilian support to enable this, at his speech to the annual Veterans for Peace gathering in Seattle on August 12, 2006:

> I speak with you about a radical idea . . . The idea is this: that to stop an illegal and unjust war, the soldiers can choose to stop fighting it . . . Those wearing the uniform must know beyond any shadow of a doubt that by refusing immoral and illegal orders they will be supported by the people not with mere words but by action . . . To support the troops who resist, you must make your voices heard. If they see thousands supporting me, they will know. I have seen this support with my own eyes . . . For me it was a leap of faith. For other soldiers, they do not have that luxury. They must know it and you must show it to them. Convince them that no matter how long they sit in prison, no matter how long this country takes to right itself, their families will have a roof over their heads, food in their stomachs, opportunities and education.[110]

For refusing to deploy to the illegal war in Iraq and for engaging in free speech, Lt. Watada already faces a maximum of eight years in jail for a series of charges, including: missing movement, contempt toward officials (saying Bush lied about the war), and conduct unbecoming an officer and a gentleman (speaking out against illegal war). To counter this kind of crackdown, we can, as Lt Watada explains, build support "not with mere words but by action" in our communities and in antiwar and counterrecruitment movements that will help to take a stand or refuse deployment.

Resist the draft and draft registration by supporting young men who refuse to register for the selective service and preparing for mass resistance to a possible draft

If our counterrecruitment efforts successfully cut into the military's recruitment numbers, it could mean the government will have to bring back a standard military draft, "national service," or a special medical-worker draft, all of which may open a space for massive public resistance.

According to 1980 draft registration resister and current antidraft organizer Ed Hasbrouck, massive draft registration non cooperation may have been key in preventing a draft over the last the twenty-five years. He said the last General Accounting Office audit of the Selective Service found that they did not have current information on the whereabouts of as many as 75 percent of potential draftees.

We can begin educating medical professionals, who may be the most likely to be drafted, and young draft-age and younger men about the possibility of a draft and how to resist it. Instead of waiting until draft induction begins, peace-and-justice groups and individuals can begin now to help make a draft unworkable later. Young men can refuse to register, refuse to tell the selective service their whereabouts when they move, and urge their parents or those at the registration address (if you did register) not to accept or sign for an induction or other Selective Service notice, or give out any information about current whereabouts. People who did register can actively publicize their commitment to refuse a military draft.

Together counterrecruitment, GI resistance, and draft registration resistance can cut off the supply of troops and help to stop wars for empire. However, to be effective we also have to be prepared for U.S. military innovations that circumvent the need for conventional military troops. These innovations include the following:

- Privatization of the military—mercenary and private corporations getting paid for traditional military roles.
- Increased mechanization of war, or air wars and bombing campaigns that involve fewer troops and

On August 11th 2006, after being AWOL from the military for over 14 months, US Army Interrogator Sgt. Ricky Clousing spoke publicly about what he called "the daily devastation of occupation in Iraq" which led to his decision to leave his unit after completion of his tour in Iraq. He then turned himself over to military custody. On October 11th he was found guilty of AWOL and sentenced to three months in prison. Photo by Jeff Paterson, Jeff.Paterson.net

Iraq era veteran and GI resister Pablo Paredes and Fernando Suraez de Solar, father of soldier killed in Iraq, lead the Latino March for Peace and for immigrant rights in Watsonville, CA. The march went from Tijuana, Mexico to San Francisco, California.
Photo by Jeff Paterson, Jeff.Paterson.net

reduce U.S. military deaths, though often resulting in more civilian deaths among the targeted country or area.

- Recruitment, training, funding, arming, and directing of proxy armies, guerrillas, terrorist groups and death squads to do U.S. bidding without involving large numbers of U.S. troops—examples include the anti-Soviet guerrilla Army in Afghanistan in the late 1970s and 1980s, and the "Contra" Army against Nicaragua in the 1980s.
- Use of clandestine or CIA operations to disrupt, repress, or destroy governments, movements, organizations, and individuals the United States government objects to.

We can prepare for these other forms of war and intervention that do not rely on large numbers of troops by breaking out of the limitations of single issue organizing. If we educate ourselves, our groups, our communities, the public and our movements about the history of United States interventions and war, we will see why it is important not to organize simply against a particular war, like Iraq, or a particular component of militarism, like recruitment. We can't afford to create new organizations or movements every time the government finds new ways to assert its policies of war for empire.

Many groups and movements develop an understanding of underlying systemic problems and include them in their goals and mission statements, so it is not a stretch when the U.S. government wages war on another country or resorts to forms of intervention that do not depend on troops. For example the GI Resister support group Courage to Resist, instead of just opposing the Iraq war and occupation, has adopted a mission statement that includes opposition to "war and occupation and the policies of empire."

Pillar of War: Corporate Profiteers

Another of the most obvious pillars of war are the corporations that play an essential role in the Iraqi occupation, and in the motives behind it. Corporations are essential to continuing the war and occupation in Iraq. Forcing them to withdraw their participation would shut down essential components of and motives for the war and occupation—while opening up tremendous opportunities to Iraqis to define and create their own economic future.

There are four main types of corporate involvement in the war and occupation:

- "Reconstruction" contractors, like Parsons, with $5.3 billion in reconstruction contracts that include $243 million for the construction of 150 health care centers. More than two years into the work and $186 million spent, just six centers have been built, only two of which are treating patients.
- Privatizers, the corporations that are working toward privatizing Iraq's economy, such as Chevron Texaco, which is poised to reap trillions of dollars off of Iraq's oil sector.
- Weapons and military supply manufacturers, like Lockheed-Martin, that have seen their stock value and profits skyrocket since the "War on Terror" began.
- Mercenary "private security" corporations that provide logistics and services, like CACI International, which provides interrogators, including those involved in Abu Ghraib torture.

Campaigns targeting corporate profiteers are gaining momentum. The Bay Area's Direct Action to Stop the War targeted the San Francisco–based Bechtel Corporation in 2003–2004 after the company received an early Iraq reconstruction contract. Protestors emphasized that not only

Iraq era veteran and GI resister Pablo Paredes leads the Latino March for Peace and for immigrant rights in Salins, CA. The march went from Tijuana, Mexico to San Francisco, California. Photo by Jeff Paterson, Jeff.Paterson.net

COURAGE TO RESIST!
THE WAR
PEREGRINACIÓN POR LA PAZ
MARCH FOR PEACE
Por la Paz

did the company receive its contract without competition, but that it ultimately received nearly $3 billion for work that absolutely could and should have been done by Iraqis themselves, and with far better results. Bechtel's inability to restore water, electricity, or sewage to even pre-war levels significantly contributed to anger—and likely violent resistance to—the occupation and the soldiers enforcing it. Hundreds of protestors repeatedly blockaded the entrances to Bechtel's headquarters while delivering scathing critiques of the company's performance in Iraq. Unable to endure the constant attention, Bechtel executives decided not to bid on any new work in Iraq after their initial two contracts.

In Houston, Texas, activists organized a grassroots campaign to raise awareness about Halliburton's complicity in the occupation of Iraq, which included two large scale nonviolent direct actions at the company's 2004 and 2005 shareholder meetings.

Houston Global Awareness, the lead organizing group, said in its call to action, "Halliburton is essential to continuing the war and occupation in Iraq and forcing them to withdraw their participation would shut down essential parts and motives for the war and occupation. Not only are their operations in Iraq depriving the children and people of Iraq of any sort of future, but also the billions upon billions in no-bid contracts heaped upon them by George Bush and Dick Cheney results in the further weakening of social services here at home."

These protests increased the chorus of resistance to Halliburton's obscene profits and poor performance in Iraq. The company is now being investigated under dozens of charges by government agencies and, most significantly, has lost its largest U.S. government contract in 2006 for logistical support for U.S. troops. The contract is now being competitively bid.

The power of corporate profiteers can be weakened through aggressive and innovative anti-corporate campaigns. These campaigns create an economic, political and social cost to war profiteering, until they are forced to pull out.

Corporate Media

Corporate media's steady stream of lies, distortions, and repetition of the United States government "war on terror" rhetoric was essential in propagating the pretense for the invasion of Iraq and is key to maintaining some level of public support for the war and occupation. If people were given the right information, they would be more likely, and better equipped, to resist. Independent Iraq and Middle East journalist Dahr Jamail explains that creating reliable independent media and optimizing access to it "will be a better path to ending the occupation than continuing to react to the disinformation and the lies put out by the corporate media and the Bush administration."

We can weaken this pillar by creating and supporting independent media and running media accountability campaigns to educate the public to become critical of media bias, and to curb some of the most outrageous lies and distortions. Additionally, independent media advocacy campaigns could set goals of switching over large numbers of people from watching/listening/reading corporate media to watching/listening/reading more alternative media. Groups can pressure local radio and television to carry syndicated independent media programs like Democracy Now! and Free Speech Radio News. Imagine if switching to independent media sources had been a key component of all the antiwar organizing over the last few years.

For example, a local group could pick one local TV station and monitor the experts and opinions about the Iraq war over one month. They could very publicly demand, in a country split on the issue, that the station have balanced war coverage with equal numbers of pro- and antiwar experts and opinions. This could include public education, letter-writing and phone-call campaigns, meetings with producers, petitions calling for balanced coverage, and pledges to switch to independent media if the station does not meet the demand for balanced war coverage.

Successful alternative media campaigns act to give people all the information they need to understand their world, and decide for themselves how to participate in it.

Achieving Fundamental Change

To stop the next war—be it in Iran, North Korea, Syria, Venezuela, or elsewhere—and to counter the domestic impact of the policies of empire (of which the Iraq war and occupation are symptoms), it is essential that we think and frame our campaigns and education within its systemic context. In this way our efforts to stop the Iraq war will be complementary and cumulative rather than competitive and fractured, and will build momentum towards stopping other wars and injustices without having to start new movements each time.

Importantly, we must articulate positive, directly democratic, socially just, ecological alternatives. When we oppose oil companies like Chevron Texaco, we must simultaneously advocate alternative fuel/transportation systems and democratic non-corporate institutions to take their place. When we call for soldiers to refuse deployment, we must build supportive communities for them to join instead. When we expose the lies of corporate media, we must provide alternative sources. This "saying yes as loudly as we say no" will help the movement we are building to continue on long after we have stopped the occupation of Iraq.

A final key ingredient for a successful strategy is our ability to frame our own struggles, or tell our own story. If we are acting defensively within the framework of the United States government and their "war on terror" story, we will always be on the defensive. If we allow them to define reality, we will always lose. If we limit ourselves to defensively arguing that there are no nuclear weapons in Iraq, for example, without challenging the legitimacy and cost of the U.S. being an empire, then we are operating in a reality defined by those in power. We have to be able to understand, fight and win the "battle of the story."

The courage of young people in the military, on the campuses and in the streets are showing us how to assert our people power. It's clear that more and more folks in the U.S. and around the world have the courage to resist. Can we can find what lies in the root of the word courage—le coeur, or heart—to assert our power as communities, as movements and as people to reverse the policies of empire and build a better world?

Photo by Jeff Paterson, Jeff.Paterson.net

Photo by Jeff Paterson, Jeff.Paterson.net

TOOLS FOR EFFECTIVE ORGANIZING

The following exercises can be used to help develop your group's analysis and strategy in order to effectively organize for change.

Spectrum of Allies

This exercise can make it clear that we don't have to change our opponent or our entire society to achieve some of our goals. It can help people narrow their focus on key groups involved in the issue and narrow it down to a manageable and strategic campaign. This exercise come from Martin Oppenheimer and George Lakey's classic book, *A Manual for Direct Action* (Quadrangle Books, 1965).

How to Facilitate

Introduce: Use newsprint to describe the idea that in most social change situations there is a struggle between those who want the change and those who don't. Those who do are represented by a point at one side of the newsprint (say, on the left) and the opponents by a point at the other side. Explain that societies (or towns, states, corporations, school boards, and so on) usually include a range of groups that can be put on kind of spectrum from closest to the point of view of the advocates to farthest away, and draw a horizontal line to represent that.

Spectrum chart: Then draw a halfmoon or half of a pie with wedges with those who want change and their opponents on either side. Ask for an example of an issue people in the group might be working on. Suggest a demand the advocates might have (say, limiting military recruiters access to students at school) and ask who in society might be inclined to be most supportive, least supportive, and in the middle. Solicit examples: teachers unions? parents groups? antiwar groups? veteran organizations? etc. As the participants identify groups and location on the spectrum, write them into the "pie." Do this only enough to make the idea clear.

Reflect: Give the good news: in most social change campaigns it's not necessary to win the opponent to your point of view, even if the opponent is the power holders. It's only necessary to move each of the pie wedges one step in your direction. Pause to make sure that's clear. Then complicate the picture slightly: sometimes polarization happens, and the wedges closest to the opponent move away from you and toward the opponent. You can still win, if enough of society takes a step in your direction.

Let the group digest the good news for a bit; let it sink in that activists often have the mistaken idea that they need to win everyone (inviting despair), or that their whole attention needs to be on the power holders (again inviting despair).

Apply: At this point you can ask everyone to take a piece of paper and draw out a spectrum of allies pie wedge for their particular issue or campaign, placing all the key groups on the chart. A second question may be, "If we have limited time and capacity what are two key groups we can try to move?" Then ask, "What are two things we can do to try to move each of those two groups?" And finally ask, "Could this work as an initial campaign?"

Discuss: Create small groups for discussion or keep together as a large group. If a variety of issues are present in the group, they could form issue groups to compare notes. Let them work for a while (keeping track of their work), then ask them to brainstorm tactics that might effectively communicate with the wedges that they want most to win as allies.

Lessons: Ask the groups for what they learned and their reflections: Write it up on newsprint. Emphasize points like this: it's a huge win if you can get a group that was slightly hostile to move into neutrality. It's a huge win if you can get the group/wedge next to your end of the spectrum to move into activism with you. It's usually not necessary to move the opponents a step toward you in order to win, although it can hasten the win.

Steps of a Direct Action Campaign

This exercise can help a group to understand the stages of an action or campaign, and how to plan one. This basic action campaign model is adapted from one used by the civil rights movement in the 1960s. These stages of a direct action campaign are not separate entities to be worked through one by one. The campaign is ongoing and once a stage has begun it should continue throughout the campaign. If a campaign is already underway this model can help identify what stage the campaign is at and it's never too late to go back work on earlier stages.

Long-Term Goals

These may be both the long-term goals of a specific campaign—like higher wages, stopping a toxic facility in a neighborhood, or removing a dictator—and also the longer term systemic goals of the social change movements—the transformation of society, its values, and a positive vision of a future world. For example, an antiwar group may

Oakland, CA. © 2005 David Hanks, www.davidhanks.org

have as it's long-term goal to stop the U.S. war in Iraq, but may also have longer-term goals to eliminate empire or corporate capitalism and/or to create directly democratic, just, ecological alternatives.

▶ **What are the long-term goals of the campaign?**

1.
2.

more . . .

▶ **Short-Term Goals**

Short-term, winnable goals that can be achieved along the way to the long-term ones are key to the success of a campaign. They should be achievable in the not-too-far future to provide a boost, encouragement, and milestone on the way toward the long-term goals. They should be measurable so you know when you have accomplished them (and have a victory party!). They should also be a significant step toward realizing your longer-term goals.

▸ What are the short-term goals of the campaign?

1.
2.

more . . .

▸ Investigate

Goals:

- Get the facts: understand the nature and extent of the problem.
- Understand how it affects us/other communities/people/environment?
- Find out who has the power to do what related to the problem/solution.

▸ What needs to be investigated/researched? What information do we need?

1.
2.
3.

more . . .

▸ Education

Methods: Door-to-door canvas, leafletting at shopping center/public places/events, letters to the editor, street theater, a press conference, a teach-in, posters, a web site, articles, a petition, a letter to officials, brochures and newsletters, and the like.

Goals:

- Inform the community/public; bring about public discussion and concern.
- Garner support for the campaign.
- Put pressure on the opponent to make changes.

People shut down and repaint recruitment center and occupy street in front. Oakland, CA. 2005

Photo © 2005 David Hanks, www.davidhanks.org

How will you educate the community/public?

1.
2.
3.

more . . .

Negotiate

Goals:

- Give the opponent a clear, documented, and publicized opportunity to resolve the conflict.
- Possibly achieve resolution of conflict.
- Inform the community/public; bring about public discussion and concern.
- Get support for the campaign.
- Put pressure on the opponent to make changes.

How will you negotiate, and with whom?

1.
2.

more . . .

Demonstrate

Methods: Informational picket, march, street theater, rally, vigil, human billboard, and so on.

Goals:

- Inform the community/public; bring about public discussion and concern.
- Get support for the campaign.
- Increase pressure on the opponent to make changes.

How will you demonstrate?

1.
2.
3.

more . . .

Direct Action

Methods: Sit-in, boycott, walkout, occupation, strike, blockade, and the like.

Goals:

- Inform the community/public; bring about public discussion and concern.
- Garner support for the campaign.
- Increase pressure on the opponent to make changes.
- Create a "crisis" to force the public and your opponent to address the issue and move supporters to be more involved.
- Dramatize the conflict in a way that explains your side.
- Show the depth of your commitment and test the determination of your opponent.
- Spark actions and campaigns elsewhere.

How will you take direct action?

1.
2.
3.

more . . .

Protracted Struggle

Methods: Continued and escalated negotiation, education, demonstration, and direct action.

Goals:

- Inform the community/public; bring about public discussion and concern.
- Get support for the campaign.
- Increase pressure on the opponent to make changes.
- Sustain the campaign until the injustice is eliminated.
- Build new institutions to replace the inadequate or unjust ones.

To Amerika on the Evening After the 2,000th US Death

By Jeremy Shenk

This day is no different then yesterday.
Even though it might feel that way.
There is no significance to this day any more than any other day.
People die every day. Soldiers, civilians, people die every day.
Capitalism kills every day through starvation, through the gun, through the sick amounts of wealth being concentrated in the hands of the few.

I am angry today but no more than yesterday
Because when was the 2,000th Iraqi killed?
I don't even fucking remember.
Because they try and teach me that our troops are different from their troops when its just kids from my neighborhood fighting kids from other neighborhoods a lot like mine.
They try and teach us not to care what happens to Iraqis.

And Amerika, I don't know what to do about you anymore.
You broke my heart so many times.
I want to be angry, but I just feel sad.
That the country I live in is such a force for death and destruction and capital over human need.
I want to be angry because I can't be sad.
Because sadness leads to despair and despair

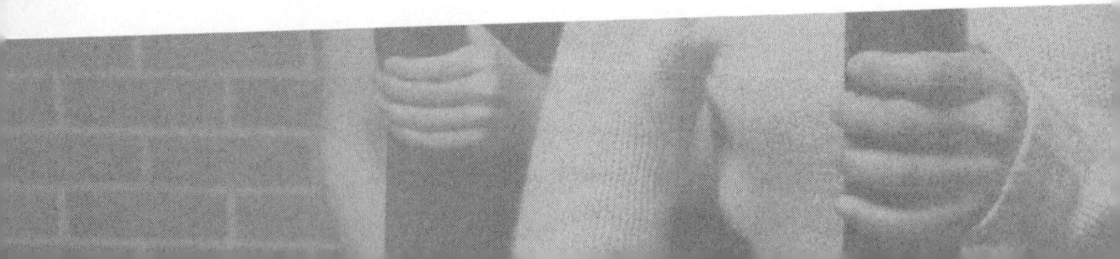

leads to complacency and
complacency leads to our
paralysis which means
more havoc will be reaped
all over the world by this
government.

Amerika, we're breaking
up.
I am through with you and
your false promises being
told to get kids to sign up
and go die for a lie.
I am through with your
Halliburtons your DeLays
and your Wallmarts.
1 Death for a lie is too
many.
These 2,000 US deaths for
a lie are too many.
I am done with you
Amerika.
See but I won't leave.
Oh no, I won't leave you
alone.
I will be that annoying ex
partner that follows you
around and ruins your new
relationships.
Or calls you drunk at 4
AM
Or comes and yells at you
at your job.
I will be the thorn in your
side Amerika.
I will resist
We must resist.
Because we can do better.
The world doesn't have to
look like this.
The place we live doesn't
have to be like this.

We have to know that in
times like these with 2,000
dead US soldiers and
100,000 dead Iraqis that
this can stop.
And more importantly
that we can stop it.
We can shut this war
down.
We can shut down
recruitment.
We have power and we
must use it.

So if you wanna love, then
love.
If you wanna pray, then
pray.

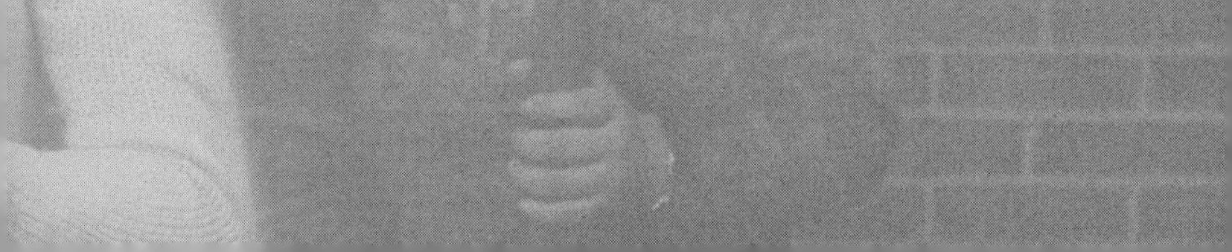

If you wanna sing, then
sing.

But if you feeling like me
and wanna yell, then yell.
And if you wanna scream,
then scream
If you wanna march, then
march.
And if you wanna burn
then fucking burn.

Because I'm burning.
Iraq is burning.
The Global South is
burning with Resistance
And which side are we on?
Because we can't be
neutral in times such as
these.
Neutrality is picking the
side of US Imperialism
and I pick the side of
resistance.
The side of those who
are working to create the
world they want to live in.
A world where we will
dance on the ruins of
capitalism
and know that we have
more in common with
Iraqis than we got with
Bush

Now is the time!
To let the fire in our hearts
become the scream in our
throats and the drumbeat
of our footsteps as we walk
the path to a new world.
Revolution is a process and
we can start that today.
Because elsewhere it has
been started without us.
We can march in step with
the kids in Toledo, the
Zapatistas of Mexico, the
farmers of Brazil, renters
in S. Africa, our sisters in
Afghanistan, the workers
of S. Korea, and people
over the world.
The movement is moving
and the world is changing!

And where will we say we
were when the earth took a

turn for the better?
Where were you when the people of the world started to
win?

I don't want to see it happen on my TV I want to see
it and be in it on the streets of Pittsburgh in our
every day resistance.
Because all Power, comes through the People.
And we are the People.

They say the heart is a muscle the size of your fist
So we say today, to keep on loving and keep on fighting.

Photos: Geoff Oliver Bugbee

▸ **How can the campaign escalate its tactics and broaden its support?**

1.
2.

more . . .

▸ **What alternative institution/s could be built to replace the existing one?**

1.
2.

more . . .

The Battle of the Story Worksheet

From smartMeme Training and Strategy Project

This exercise is intended to help grassroots activists create more compelling narratives to communicate their campaigns. The Battle of the Story is the framework through which we can analyze the current media climate around an issue—whether it's the story that the power-holders are telling about the issue or just the accepted status-quo perception. The worksheet asks you to apply three different elements of story telling (conflict, sympathetic characters, and show don't tell) to both the power holder's story and then our story as grassroots activists. Once you have articulated these elements, use the logic of the story to identify the assumptions that allow each of the stories to operate. The final row of the chart—the points of intervention—is the place to identify weaknesses in each story and rhetorical strategies for challenging each story's assumptions. This could take the form of challenging the story's framing, contrasting alternate visions of the future, articulating hopes, dispelling fears, or exposing hidden agendas. At the completion of this exercise you should be able to revisit each story's core messages in terms of headlines and sound bytes and see how they need to be adjusted to help win the Battle of the Story!

Story

Answer the following for both of the following Power Holders/Status-quo and Change Agents in each category. Do it with a group and write it up on big paper with markers.

Conflict

How is the problem being framed? Who is the conflict between? Who are the good guys and the bad guys? Identify the conflict you want to highlight. Like any Hollywood blockbuster, social change movements are fraught with seat-gripping conflict and drama. We must be certain we are defining these stakes in our terms with our language.

Power Holders/Status-quoting Agents
Sympathetic Characters

Who are the victims? Who are the messengers that tell the story? Cast the sympathetic characters involved in your story. Pay close attention to who is receiving top billing as the messenger. Who are our heroes? Who are their villains? Frequently the messenger is as compelling and powerful as the message, so choose carefully.

Show Don't Tell

How does the story use images or anecdotes to convince without being preachy? How does the story engage our values and encourage us to choose sides? Nobody likes to be spoonfed a worldview. People believe inherently in the right to make up their own minds. We need to become increasingly savvy about appealing to people's values. A question is often times more powerful than a statement because it forces the audience to engage. Likewise, speaking in terms of values doesn't mean using the self-righteous political rhetoric of right and wrong, it means connecting our issues to the bigger concerns that shape people's lives.

Assumptions

What are the unstated assumptions? What does someone have to believe to accept the story?

Points of Intervention

How can we challenge the other story's assumptions? What are the other story's vulnerabilities? Limits? Contradictions? Lies?

Offer Vision

Our stories must articulate an alternative and more compelling vision. The visions articulated by progressives are too often steeped in the "sky's falling" metaphor. Problem is, the sky is still up there and people are tired of hearing that from us. People don't want to think problems are insolvable. Society's fear of a vacuum often leads us to choose familiar evils over unknowns. It is up to us to provide the vision that makes the unknown alternatives real. The good news is we know there are solutions that work —not only technical solutions like anti-pollution scrubbers in smokestacks, but policy solutions like getting money out of politics, and systemic solutions like building grassroots movements for real democracy. It is not enough for our side just to criticize: people need to have tangible opportunities to engage not only their minds, but also their hearts and their hands in building alternatives. It isn't enough to tear down the world, we must offer up what we would build in its place. Don't stop there, though! In order to win the Battle of the Story we must also understand and challenge the power holder's stories. The first step in retaking control of the narrative is to diligently compare our story with the one we are battling. There are critical lessons inherent in this exercise.

Spoken word poet reads to people before counter-recruitment march and direct action. Oakland, CA.
© 2005 David Hanks, www.davidhanks.org

Oakland, CA, 2005
© 2005 David Hanks, www.davidhanks.org

Chevron
Gasoline
Self Serve
REGULAR UNLEADED
PLUS UNLEADED
Chevron
PEOPLE POWER CAN END THE WAR

CONCLUSION

Our own generation is in a long war against a determined enemy.
—George W. Bush, 2006 State of the Union Speech

We cannot have peace if we are only concerned with peace. War is not an accident. It is the logical outcome of a certain way of life. If we want to attack war, we have to attack that way of life.
—A.J. Muste

To win a better world, we have to look, think, and act beyond the next action, meeting, public hearing, or campaign. We have to actually envision, plan for, act on—and perhaps most difficult—believe in a future without war and the political and economic systems that create it. War and militarism are not inevitable—counterrecruitment offers a glimpse into an alternate future for youth and our country in which we aren't pushed and pulled to war. Counterrecruitment is a long-term strategy and commitment to undermine the military's effort to legitimize war, coerce enlistment, and seep into the civilian institution of public school. Its very act rejects militarism as a way of life. Every time a conversation or action, big or small, helps a young person hungry for opportunities, independence, or respect see his or her future without the military, we win. Done thousands of times, it is the basis of a powerful movement.

We have an urgent need to believe in and take action towards a future without war. The United States government recently funded a study on alternative futures for the U.S. Empire. The "Alternative Futures and Army Force Planning Implications for the Future Force Era" study by the Rand Corporation creates six distinct U.S. military combat scenarios in the year 2025.[111] Each future requires a massive military to maintain United States global dominance. Their next to worst scenario, "Transnational Web," is one which "witnesses a dramatic growth in the threat to the United States presented by radical transnational 'peace and social justice' groups. Using the goal of creating a just 'global civil society' as their rallying cry, large militant transnational actors appear, promoting radical agendas for the environment, nuclear disarmament, and Third World land reform." In this scenario, military strategies for countering them are necessary.

As an alternative to the grim futures that promote militarism, war, ecological disaster, and human suffering, leading thinkers are offering economic, political, and social systems that make war obsolete. For example, Brian Martin gives an example of a viable alternative framework to military conflict in his book *Social Defense, Social Change*: "The idea of social defense—namely of abolishing military forces and relying in their stead on nonviolent struggles by the general population—is extremely radical. Social defense is not just a defense option. It is a direction for action that should be known to all those who seek a society without oppression, inequality, or violence."

Counterrecruitment captures imagination and helps people find an alternative future they can believe in. We draw inspiration from thinkers like John Michael Greer, a practicing mage, who wrote a reflection on the book *Globalize Liberation:*

> The point I'd like to make, once you've tried on both stories of the future, is that both of them—the story of corporate triumph and the story of corporate failure—explain the past and present equally well. Which of these stories is true? Wrong question. The events that define either story haven't happened yet, and which story people believe could well determine which way the ending turns out. If people believe that the global corporate system is invulnerable, most of them will make their peace with it and come to rely on it, and their actions will give it more power. If people believe that the global corporate system is doomed, most of them will withdraw their support from it and begin seeking alternatives—and that in itself could doom it. Ask yourself, then, which of these stories fosters more hope, gives more encouragement to alternative visions of society, and more effectively cuts at the mental foundations of today's economic and political systems?[112]

Army of None helps to tell an alternative future of peace, of opportunity, and of hope. The future of people and our planet depends on us.

Oakland, CA, 2005

RESOURCES

Best places to get up-to-date fliers and background information:

■ www.projectyano.org
The Project on Youth and Nonmilitary Opportunities (YANO). Comprehensive source for fliers and resources in English and Spanish. Includes students'-rights handout and background information. Contact this San Diego–based organization for specific contacts in southern California—but this network also has its finger on the pulse of nationwide activities.

■ www.militaryfreeschools.org
The Coalition Against Militarism in Our Schools (CAMS). Excellent resource with Adopt A School toolkit to walk you through organizing counterrecruitment actions. Successful organization that models counter-recruitment practices.

■ www.comdsd.org
Committee Opposed to Militarism and the Draft (COMD). Outstanding resource for fliers and archived newsletter for the latest in legislation, counterrecruitment, and youth work. Includes great models shown for district policy on equal access for counterrecruiters and limiting military recruiter access to students.

Best place to find other counterrecruiter partners and allies:

TIP: Search the Yahoo.com groups page with "counter-recruitment" and you'll find over twenty local online groups discussing counterrecruitment.

■ www.ivaw.org
Iraq Veterans Against the War (IVAW). Excellent resource to locate veterans to speak in local schools and at community events.

Best counterrecruitment how-to guides:

■ www.trainingforchange.org
Training for Change (TFC). *Before You Enlist and After You Say No: AFSC's Counterrecruitment Training Manual,* which includes group exercises, complete workshops, curriculum, and other resources for counterrecruitment organizers.

■ www.warresisters.org
The War Resisters' League (WRL). WRL is an eighty-three-year-old organization that has revitalized its counterrecruitment efforts nationwide. It has created one of the best guides to counterrecruitment written for youth. The graphics and message are very now. For a few dollars you can order *DMZ: A Guide to Taking Your School Back from the Military.*

■ www.counterrecruitmentguide.org
The New Yorker's Guide to Military Recruitment. According to the web site, "This free sixty-four-page, pocket-sized book includes everything a New Yorker needs to know about military recruitment and resources for counterrecruitment in NYC. Profiles of former soldiers sit side-by-side with information on the enlistment contract,

military myths, the No Child Left Behind Act, action/legal resources, a Harper's-style index of facts, and much more. At the heart of the book is an opt-out form that students can tear out, fill in, and hand over to their school administrators to prevent their contact information from being released to recruiters." This is an excellent guide to counterrecruitment that can be adapted to your state. Download the guide or order a copy. It's one of the best.

■ www.notyoursoldier.org
Best counterrecruitment video, available online as a Flash animation. A must see. Not Your Soldier, a coalition of groups big and small that believes that youth have the power to stop the war in Iraq, has created the hippest, most provocative online video aimed at youth. It draws from the recently released film on GI resistance during Vietnam entitled, *Sir, No Sir!*. A great tool to use in a classroom or link from your own web site.

Best place to help current military service members in crisis:

■ www.girights.org
The Central Committee for Conscientious Objectors (CCCO) is over fifty-years-old and runs a nationwide GI Rights hotline staffed by volunteers who assist service people.

■ www.couragetoresist.org
Courage to Resist is a group of concerned community members, veterans, and military families that supports military objectors to illegal war and occupation and the policies of empire.

■ www.centeronconscience.org
The Center on Conscience and War web site is an excellent resource for rules and support for conscientious

objectors—soldiers who are opposed to further participation in the military because of changed beliefs against war.

Best place to get information on draft registration and the draft:

■ www.resisters.info
Provides information, advice, fliers, draft resistance speakers, and answers to frequently asked questions about the military draft, draft registration, draft resistance, and the health care workers' draft.

Best place to find ideas and how-to's for art, theater, and cultural activities:

PUPPETS:

■ www.gis.net/~puppetco/
The Puppeteers' Cooperative home page has information and how-to's about all sorts of puppetry, theater, costume, and pageant ideas.

■ www.zeitgeist.net/wfca/handbook.html
The Wise Fool Handbook is a hundred-page booklet with detailed instructions on making masks, building giant puppets, walking on stilts, and more!

DRUMS:

■ www.puppetista.org/drums
Drumming, and making drums and other instruments for demonstrations and celebrations.

BILLBOARD ALTERATION:

■ www.geocities.com/billboardcorrections/index.html
California Department of Corrections (CDC) is a private correctional facility that protects the public through the

secure management, discipline, and rehabilitation of California's advertising. Includes how-to's and examples.

■ www.billboardliberation.com
Billboard Liberation Front (BLF): Marketing for the People. The BLF web site writes, "The procedures outlined here are based on our twenty-plus years experience executing billboard improvements professionally, safely, and (knock wood) without injury or arrest. In most cases, it should not be necessary to follow the elaborate, even obsessive precautions we outline here. A can of spray paint, a blithe spirit, and a balmy night are all you really need."

STENCILS:

■ www.spraypaintstencils.com
Spray Paint Stencils is a web site devoted to providing everyone with tons of free stencils to download, and tutorials for creating your own custom stencils.

■ www.stencilrevolution.com
Stencil gallery with great how-to tutorials and resources.

REBEL CLOWNING:

■ www.clownarmy.org
The Clandestine Insurgent Revel Clown Army writes, "We are clowns because what else can one be in such a stupid world. Because inside everyone is a lawless clown trying to escape. Because nothing undermines authority like holding it up to ridicule. Because since the beginning of time tricksters have embraced life's contradictions, creating coherence through confusion."

THEATER OF THE OPPRESSED:

■ www.theateroftheoppressed.org
Theater of the Oppressed is a system of games and special

techniques that aims at developing, in the oppressed citizens, the language of the theater, which is the essential human language.

Best place for strategy and organizing resources for groups:

■ www.smartmeme.com
The smartMeme collective is a group of change agents who work to support grassroots movements with strategy and training resources, values-based communications tools, and meme campaigning. The strategic-resources section of this book includes "Battle of the Story" and other great worksheets and essays.

■ www.peoplepowerstrategy.org
People Power Strategy Resources including essays and resources on people power antiwar strategy from the People Powered Strategy Network.

■ www.thechangeagency.org
This site provides access to resources and manuals on working with groups, strategizing, and community organizing.

■ www.trainingforchange.org
Training for Change is an activist training organization that helps groups stand up for justice, peace, and environmental harmony. The web site includes a great tools section with the Spectrum of Allies and other strategy, diversity/antioppression, team building, nonviolent action, and facilitation tools and exercises.

■ www.spinproject.org
The SPIN Project is for organizations working to build a fair, just, and equitable society that want to be heard in today's crowded media environment. The web site

includes a helpful resources/tutorial section with media basics. SPIN encourages you to develop a strategic communications infrastructure that includes building relationships with reporters, mobilizing for specific campaigns, and targeting key audiences based on your organizations' needs.

■ www.afmpgame.com
A Force More Powerful is the first and only computer game to teach the waging of conflict, resistance, and insurrection using nonviolent resistance and intervention methods.[114]

ENDNOTES

1 Jahnkow, Rick, "In Need of a Proactive Peace Movement," *Draft NOtices*, January–March 2006.

2 A pseudonym.

3 Perry, William J. and others, "The U.S. Military: Under Strain and at Risk," National Security Advisory Group, January 2006.

4 Cave, Damien, "For a General, A Tough Mission: Building the Army," *New York Times*, February 5, 2006.

5 Lardner, Richard, "Army Uses New Tactics To Meet Recruiting Goals," *Tampa Tribune*, October 7, 2006.

6 Ibid.

7 Ibid.

8 Hoffer, Jim, "Military Recruitment Abuses Uncovered," WABC, November 2, 2006m http://abclocal.go.com/wabc/story?section=investigators&id=1722401.

9 Griffin, Christopher, "Recruiters Struggle to Keep the Army from Breaking," *Armed Forces Journal*, March 2006, http://www.armedforcesjournal.com/2006/03/1814016.

10 Jahnkow, Rick, "For Those Who Believe We Need a Draft," *Draft NOtices*, September-October 2002.

11 Hegranes, Christine, "Pacifists for Warmm," *San Francisco Weekly*, November 6, 2005.

12 Dan Siegel, in discussion with the author, July 15, 2006.

13 King, Jr., Martin Luther, "Beyond Vietnam" (speech, Riverside Church, New York City, NY, April 4, 1967).

14 Butler, Smedley, *War is a Racket: The Anti-War Classic by America's Most Decorated General*, (Los Angeles: Feral House, 2003).

15 United States Department of Defense, "Defense Budget Materials: FY 2006 Budget," United States Department of Defense, http://www.dod.mil/comptroller/defbudget/fy2006/index.html.

16 Statistical Information Analysis Division, Work Force Publications, "Worldwide Manpower Distribution," SIAD, http://siadapp.dior.whs.mil/personnel/Pubs.htm#M05.

17 United States Census, "Statistical Abstract of the United States: 2004-2005, Section 10," United States Census, http://www.census.gov/prod/2004pubs/04statab/defense.pdf.

18 Chalmers Johnson, "America's Empire of Bases," TomDispatch.com, January, 15, 2004, http://www.tomdispatch.com/index.mhtml?pid=1181 (accessed Nov 20, 2006).

19 Suskind, Ron, "Without a Doubt: Faith, Certainty and the Presidency of George W. Bush," *New York Times Magazine*, October 17, 2004.
20 Martin, Brian, *Social Defense, Social Change*, (London: Freedom Press, 1993).
21 Arlene Inouye, in discussion with the author, July 15, 2006.
22 Sal was influenced by recent news reports of increased military presence and shooting of immigrants at the Mexican border as part of Operation Jump Start as reported in, "Texas Guardsmen Charged in Shooting Say They were Bored," KWTX, September 18, 2006, http://www.kwtx.com/home/headlines/3944366.html September 18, 2006 (accessed September 20, 2006).
23 U.S. Department of Defense ad campaign, "Make it a Two-Way Conversation," 2006, Today's Military, http://www.TodaysMilitary.com.
24 Cave, Damien, "Army Recruiters Say They Feel Pressure to Bend Rules," *New York Times*, May 3, 2005.
25 Cave, Damien, "Critics Say It's Time to Overhaul Army's Bonus System." *New York Times*, August 15, 2005.
26 Defense Manpower Data Center, "2002 Status of Forces Survey of Active-Duty Members, Department of Defense," July 2002, http://www.dmdc.osd.mil/surveys/survey.html (accessed November 21, 2006).
27 National Coalition for Homeless Veterans. "Most Often Asked Questions Regarding Homeless Veterans," http://www.nchv.org/background.cfm (accessed November 20, 2006).
28 Ensign, Todd, *America's Army Today: The Challenge of Militarism*, (New York: The New Press, 2004).
29 United States Department of Veterans Affairs Education web site, http://www.gibill.va.gov/education/rates/CH30/ch30rates100105.htm.
30 Cave, Damien, "Critics Say It's Time to Overhal Army's Bonus System," *New York Times*, August 15, 2005.
31 DD Form 4/1, "Enlistment/Reenlistment Document," Armed Forces of the United States.
32 Lehrer, Jim. "Challenging Orders," *Newshour with Jim Lehrer*, February 24, 2004, http://www.pbs.org/newshour/bb/military/jan-june05/stop-loss_2-24.html.
33 Benjamin, Mark, "How many have gone to war?" *Salon*, April 12, 2005, http://salon.com/news/feature/2005/04/12/troops_numbers/ (accessed November 20, 2006).
34 Moss, Michael, "Pentagon Study Links Fatalities to Body Armor," *New York Times*, January 7, 2006.
35 The New Yorkers' Guide to Military Recruitment in the 5 Boroughs, http://www.counterrecruitmentguide.org/ (accessed September 20, 2006).
36 United States Army Recruiting Command, *USAREC Pamphlet* 350–13, Sept 1, 2004.
37 Ibid.

38 White, Josh, "Violations of Military Recruiters Up Sharply," *Boston Globe*, August 15, 2005, http://www.washingtonpost.com/wp-dyn/content/article/2006/08/14/AR2006081401002.html (accessed November 20, 2006).

39 A pseudonym.

40 Garcia, Sal, in discussion with the author, July 13 2006.

41 American Friends Service Committee's Youth & Militarism Program, "Trading Books for Soldiers: The True Cost of JROTC," *Peacework*, October 2004, http://afsc.org/pwork/0410/041021.htm (accessed November 20, 2006).

42 Central Committee for Conscientious Objectors, "JROTC Wastes Scarce Funds," *Questioning JROTC*, August 10, 2006, http://www.objector.org/jrotc/jrotcfunds.html (accessed November 20, 2006).

43 Ibid.

44 Cardoso, Dayana, in discussion with the author, July 18, 2006.

45 Central Committee for Conscientious Objectors. "JROTC Wastes Scarce Funds," *Questioning JROTC*, August 10, 2006, http://www.objector.org/jrotc/jrotcfunds.html (accessed November 20, 2006).

46 Bedell, Nancy, "Information about the Junior Reserve Officer Training Corps (JROTC) in the Grand Rapids Public School District," *Media Mouse Independent Media*, July 25, 2006, http://www.mediamouse.org/features/072506infor.php (accessed November 20, 2006).

47 Inuoye, Arlene, "Kick the Military out of Your School! We did it in LA and So Can You!" *Dynamic Magazine*, August 10, 2006, http://www.yclusa.org/article/articleview/1690/1/302/ (accessed November 20, 2006).

48 Central Committee for Conscientious Objectors. "JROTC Wastes Scarce Funds," *Questioning JROTC*, August 10, 2006, http://www.objector.org/jrotc/jrotcfunds.html (accessed November 20, 2006).

49 Ibid.

50 Ibid.

51 Ibid.

52 Phoebus, Jennifer, "Adopt a School," *Soldiers*, September 1994, http://www.army.mil/soldiers/sept94/p35.html.

53 Koh, Lynn, "A Movement to End Militarism," *War Times*, June 15, 2006, http://www.war-times.org/issues/WT_projectyano.htm (accessed November 20, 2006).

54 Yellow Dog Dem Woman, "Marines Recruiting 8-Year-Olds," RINF.com, http://www.rinf.com/columnists/news/marines-recruiting-8-year-olds (accessed September 23, 2006).

55 "Young Marines Fact Sheet," Young Marines, http://www.youngmarines.com/ (accessed September 24, 2006).

56 Advancement Project in collaboration with Padres and Jovenes Unidos, Southwest Youth Collaborative, and Children & Family Justice Center of Northwestern University School of Law, *Education on Lockdown: The Schoolhouse to Jailhouse Track*, http://www.advancementproject.org//reports/FINALEOLrep.pdf (accessed September 24, 2006).

57 Young Marines, http://www.youngmarines.com (accessed September 23, 2006).
58 Yellow Dog Dem Woman, "Marines Recruiting 8-Year-Olds," RINF.com, http://www.rinf.com/columnists/news/marines-recruiting-8-year-olds (accessed September 23, 2006).
59 National Center for Educational Statistics web site, "2006 report," http://nces.ed.gov/ (accessed November 21, 2006).
60 Inouye, Arlene, "Standing Up to Military Recruiters," *Rethinking Schools*, Spring 2006, http://www.rethinkingschools.org/archive/20_03/mili203.shtml (accessed August, 2006).
61 Ferner, Mike, "Pentagon Database Leaves No Child Alone," *Counterpunch*, February 4 and 5, 2006, http://counterpunch.org/ferner0204200.html (accessed August, 2006).
62 United States Army Recruiting Command, *USAREC Pamphlet* 350–13, Sept 1, 2004.
63 Jahnkow, Rick, "Beyond Opt-out," *Draft NOtices*, July-August 2005.
64 Whitehurst, Teresa, "Military Recruiting on Channel One," *CounterPunch*, February 21, 2005, http://www.counterpunch.org/whitehurst02212005.html (accessed July 2006).
65 Whitehurst, Teresa, "Military Recruiting on Channel One," *CounterPunch*, February 21, 2005, http://www.counterpunch.org/whitehurst02212005.html (accessed July 2006).
66 Bender, Bryan, "Some See Army Pitch in Preteen magazine," *Boston Globe*, July 3, 2006.
67 Goldin, Greg, "Selling War," *LA Weekly*, March 6, 2003, http://www.laweekly.com/general/features/selling-war/3068/ (accessed September 24, 2006).
68 Ibid.
69 Rampton, Sheldon, "War is Fun as Hell," *CommonDreams.org*, July 30, 2006, http://www.counterpunch.org/rampton07302005.html (accessed 9/15/2006).
70 Ibid.
71 "Simulation Learning Leader Contributes Serious Gaming Expertise and Proven Military Track Record," 3Dsolve Inc, September 20, 2006.
72 http://www.americasarmy.com/army/ (accessed September 23, 2006).
73 Rampton, Sheldon, "War is fun as Hell," *CommonDreams.org*, July 30, 2006, http://www.counterpunch.org/rampton07302005.html (accessed 9/15/2006).
74 "Hooah!" *Event*, January 21, 2006, http://www.eventmarketer.com/viewmedia.asp?prmMID=475&prmID=32# (accessed August 20, 2006).
75 U.S. General Accounting Office report GAO-03-1005, "Military Recruiting: DOD Needs to Establish Objectives and Measures to Better Evaluate Advertising's Effectiveness," U.S. General Accounting Office, http://www.gao.gov/htext/d031005.html.
76 SourceWatch Center for Media and Democracy, "Edward Bernays," http://www.sourcewatch.org/indes.php?title=edward_bernays (accessed August 20, 2006).

77 SourceWatch Center for Media and Democracy, "Walter Lippmann," http://www.sourcewatch.org/index.php?title=Walter_Lipman (accessed August 20, 2006).

78 Wiggins, Bryan K. and others, "JAMRS Report No. 2005-02: Military Knowledge Study: Measuring Military Knowledge and Examining its Relationship with Youth Propensity," Joint Advertising Market Research and Studies (JAMRS), September 2005.

79 Leo, John, "New Slogan Belies What the Army Really Is," *Jewish World Review*, #21, 2001, http://www.jewishworldreview.com/cols/leo011601.asp.

80 Ewen, Stewart, "Builders and Titans," *Time*, December 7, 1998, http://www.time.com/time/time100/builder/profile/burnett2.html.

81 Caldera, Louis, "News Transcript," United States Department of Defense, January 10, 2001, http://www.defenselink.mil/transcripts/2001/t01102001_t110army.html (accessed November 21, 2006).

82 Garfield, Bob, "U.S. Army Advertising is All It Can Be," *Advertising Age*, August 12, 2004.

83 Elliott, Stuart, "New battle cry: 'Army Strong,'" *New York Times* News Service, November 10, 2006, http://www.detnews.com/apps/pbcs.dll/article?AID=/20061110/BIZ/611100304/1001.

84 Thomas, Courtney, interview with Lieutenant General Robert, *Army Newswatch*, November 16, 2006.

85 Gi, Mark, "Crushing Dissent?" *Norwegianity*, November 15, 2006, http://www.norwegianity.com/ (accessed November 20, 2006).

86 Garfield, Bob, "New Army Ad is Strong—If You Totally Forget We're at War," *Advertising Age*, November 10, 2006, http://adage.com/columns/article?article_id=113151.

87 "War resistors hit back with Army satire," http://armywrong.net/ (accessed November 20, 2006).

88 "American Public Support for U.S. Military Operations from Mogadishu to Baghdad," Rand Institute, 2005.

89 Klein, Naomi, "1000 Voila Moments to Stop the War," *NoLogo*, February 27, 2004, http://www.nologo.org/newsite/detail.php?ID=149 (accessed August 20, 2006).

90 Joe, "Proposal to Include Leo Burnett as target on March 19," Students for Justice, February, 2003.

91 Venn, Chris, in discussion with the author, July 10, 2006.

92 Mariscal, Jorge, "Uncle Sam Goes to College," *Hasta la Victoria . . . siempre*, March 14, 2005, http://jorgemariscal.blogspot.com/.

93 Van Haritsma, Susan, in discussion with the author, July 16, 2006.

94 www.comdsd.org

95 Jahnkow, Rick, "Forecast: Decreased Likelihood of Draft," *The NonViolent Activist*, May-June 2004, http://www.warresisters.org/nva0504-3.htm (accessed August 20, 2006).

96 Jahnkow, Rick, "Using Equal Access to Counter Militarism in High School," http://www.projectyano.org/pdf/Equalaccess2006.pdf (accessed September 23, 2006).

97 Jahnkow, Rick, in discussion with the author, July 13, 2006.
98 Van Haitsma, Susan, in discussion with the author, 2006.
99 Skoczylas, Marie, in discussion with the author, August 20, 2006.
100 DeCoverly, Blank, "The Art and Science of Billboard Improvement," Billboard Liberation Front, http://www.billboardliberation.com/guidebook.html.
101 Conal, Robbie, "Guerrilla Etiquete + Postering Techniques," *Robbie Conal's Art Attack,* http://www.robbieconal.com/guerrilla.html (accessed 8/20/06).
102 *The Radio Factor with Bill O'Reilly,* Fox News, November 8, 2005.
103 Creitian, Todd, in discussion with the author, July 10, 2006.
104 Zlutnick, David, in discussion with the author, July 20, 2006.
105 Aranke, Sam, in discussion with the author, 2006.
106 Ibid.
107 Lombardi, Kristen, "Grandmothers of Invention," *Village Voice,* April 18, 2006.
108 Dickinson, Tim, "Dave Airhart: An Army of One," *Rolling Stone,* December 15, 2005.
109 Zeiger, David, in discussion with the author, August 20, 2006.
110 Watada, Lt. Ehren, "Soldiers Can Choose to Stop Fighting," *Truthout,* August 14, 2006.
111 Nichiporuk, Brian, "Alternative Futures and Army Force Planning Implications for the Future Force Era," Rand Corporation, 2005.
112 Greer, John Michael, "Essay on *Globalize Liberation,*" Mythic News, http://www.visionaryactivism.com/mythicnews.htm (Accessed November 20, 2006).